Composers on the Nine

Composers on the Nine

First published in 2011 by Queen's Temple Publications
Printed and bound by Caligraving Ltd

ISBN 978-0-9552473-5-4

QT125

Queen's Temple Publications, 15 Mallard Drive, Buckingham, MK18 1GJ

Distributed by Spartan Press, Strathmashie House, Laggan, Newtonmore, PH20 1BU

We are very grateful to the following publishers for permission to use extracts from the Symphonies:

SYMPHONY No. 1, Op. 22
Reproduced by kind permission of Alfred Lengnick & Co.

SYMPHONY No. 2, Op. 40
Music by Malcolm Arnold

SYMPHONY No. 3, Op. 63
Music by Malcolm Arnold

SYMPHONY No. 4, Op. 71
Music by Malcolm Arnold

SYMPHONY No. 5, Op. 74
Music by Malcolm Arnold

SYMPHONY No. 6, Op.95
Music by Malcolm Arnold

SYMPHONY No. 7, Op. 113
Music by Malcolm Arnold

SYMPHONY No. 8, Op. 121
Music by Malcolm Arnold

SYMPHONY No. 9, Op. 128
Music by Malcolm Arnold

Contents

Contributors' Biographies

Timothy Bowers is a pupil of Alan Bush and David Blake. He has taught at the Royal Academy of Music since 1979 and was elected FRAM in 2010. His list of compositions reflects a primary interest in instrumental writing within closed abstract forms. These works include twelve Sonatas, as well as chamber works, Concertos and a Symphony. He has also written nine song cycles and music for stage and documentary film.

Jude Carlton won the first Malcolm Arnold Composition Competition in 2009. He has studied with Paul Harris, Robin Holloway and Jeremy Thurlow and already has a long list of works to his name. His *Tune for Nep*, for marimba (and published by Peters), has already received a recording and critical acclaim.

Edward Gregson is a composer of international standing, whose music has been performed, broadcast, and commercially recorded worldwide. He studied composition with Alan Bush at the Royal Academy of Music winning many prizes for composition. Since then he has worked solely to commission and has written orchestral, chamber, instrumental and choral music, as well as music for the theatre, film and television.

Kenneth Hesketh began composing whilst a chorister at Liverpool Cathedral, later studying at the Royal College of Music. He attended Tanglewood in 1995 where he studied with Henri Dutilleux. He is now a professor at the Royal College of Music. He has received many commissions from major performing organisations around the world.

Nigel Hess works extensively as a composer and conductor in television, theatre and film. He has composed numerous scores for both American and British television productions and many scores for the Royal Shakespeare Company winning many awards. He has also composed much concert music, most recently his *Concerto for Piano and Orchestra* commissioned by HRH The Prince of Wales.

Jon Lord is an English composer, Hammond organist and pianist. Classically trained he is recognised for his Hammond organ blues-rock sound and for his pioneering work in fusing rock and classical forms. He is most famously co-founder member of Deep Purple. One of his finest works is the *Concerto for Group and Orchestra*, which was first performed at the Royal Albert Hall in 1969 by Deep Purple and the Royal Philharmonic Orchestra conducted by Malcolm Arnold.

John McCabe has been a prolific composer from an early age, and has worked in almost every genre, though large-scale forms lie at the heart of his catalogue with seven symphonies, twenty concertante works and four full-length ballets to his name. He has also established himself internationally as pianist. He experimented with serialism in his early career but his mature style is characterised by a dramatic post-tonalism, and vivid orchestrations.

David Matthews's many orchestral and chamber works include seven symphonies and twelve string quartets. Much of his output has been recorded on CD. He has also written books on Benjamin Britten and Michael Tippett, and numerous articles on contemporary music.

Matthew Taylor is a composer and conductor whose work has taken him to venues across the globe. His teachers include Melanie Daiken and Robin Holloway and among his large output are three symphonies, six string quartets and a large cache of chamber music. His *Fantasy on a theme of Arnold* for piano was first performed at the 2010 Malcolm Arnold Festival.

John Woolrich is a much commissioned and frequently performed composer, a creative teacher and an original programmer. He has composed music in all genres from vocal and choral to orchestral by way of instrumental music often for unusual combinations. Many of his works allude to literary or visual stimuli.

Foreword by Paul Harris

As symphonic cycles go, the Nine by Sir Malcolm Arnold represent a collection of truly enormous musical significance. Written at fairly regular intervals throughout his life they embody both his physical and mental state; they symbolize his concerns, both on philosophical matters and about current affairs and they demonstrate the control of an exceptional range of compositional techniques. I very much wanted to produce a special publication to compliment and celebrate the performances of the Nine at this years' Malcolm Arnold Festival and who better to write and share thoughts and insights on them but some fellow composers.

Thus was born *Composers on the Nine*. In inviting these ten distinguished composers to contribute I offered no instructions or restrictions as to content or length. As I had hoped, they have each responded with their very individual impressions, styles and approaches: each written with absolute honesty and profound perception. I am extremely indebted to them all.

Whether we wish to judge the Nine in relation to other symphonic cycles of the twentieth century (and if we do there is no doubt that they will be found to stand tall among them) or we simply wish to deepen our love for these highly personal, immensely inventive and intriguing works, *Composers on the Nine* will certainly play a significant role.

Paul Harris July 2011

Timothy Bowers

Malcolm Arnold's Symphonies and their Symbols

Foreword

In 1999, I received an invitation to attend the first performance of my orchestral work *Trumpet Aria with Variations* at a concert, followed by a short tour, given by the orchestra of the Bartok Institute in Miskolc, Hungary. The programme included Elgar's Cello Concerto and Malcolm Arnold's Eighth Symphony. I was thrilled to hear that Malcolm Arnold had accepted his invitation. Sadly, news arrived just before the event that he was too ill to attend. I knew a number of Arnold's works, was enthusiastic about them and had formed the impression from the symphonies that I knew (which, at that stage, did not include the later ones) that the music was an expression of the post-war era; the more sombre and turbulent moments a reminder of times past; the brighter side reflecting new hope tinged with a roguish disdain for old institutions and social norms. My cosy view, perhaps influenced by association with films such as *The Bridge on the River Kwai* and *The Sound Barrier* (which Arnold scored) was shattered by the nightmarish Eighth. It was time to explore this extraordinary music in depth, without preconceptions. An invitation to write this paper ahead of a complete performance of the Symphonies at the 2011 Malcolm Arnold Festival prompted me to study the symphonies, read about the composer, and think afresh. My journey through 'the Nine' has been a voyage of discovery, leaving me with the conviction that my first impressions had been superficial and that the cycle is one of major significance in the context of the symphonic repertoire of the Twentieth Century. The neglect of these works in the concert hall seems inexplicable.

My essay is a series of analytical commentaries on 'the Nine'. Such is the richness and complexity of these works that to perform the task properly would have taken a year of study and would run to several hundred pages. These, then, are first thoughts, but I hope that the reader will find some useful insights here. The main focus of my investigation is the conflict – as I see it – between Arnold's apparent allegiance to the mainstream 'abstract' symphonic tradition of tonal symphonic writing, and the musical elements that work against that perception.

Introduction

1 The cycle

Arnold was a prolific composer. His list of works is dominated by film scores and concert works in classical forms. It therefore seems surprising, given his gift for programmatic/descriptive writing, that he was drawn to 'abstract' music as his field. In the composer's own words:

Music appeals to me chiefly because of its abstract quality. ...For me the most worthwhile thoughts are expressed without words.[1]

The list of concert works includes twelve pieces that bear the title Symphony:[2]

Work	Key	Movements	Date	Duration
Symphony for Strings op. 13	A minor	3	1946	c 20'
Symphony No. 1 op. 22	D minor	3	1948/9	c 28'
Symphony No. 2 op. 40	Eb major	4	1953	c 30'
Toy Symphony op. 62	F major	3	1957	c 10'
Symphony No. 3 op. 63	Bb major	3*	1957	c 36'
Symphony No. 4 op. 71	F (Lydian)	4	1960	c 32'
Symphony No. 5 op. 74	E minor	4	1961	c 30'
Symphony No. 6 op. 95	A major	3+	1967	c 26'
Symphony No. 7 op. 113	F (major)	3	1973	c 39'
Symphony for Brass op. 123	(Bb major)†	4	1978	c 23'
Symphony No. 8 op. 124	D major	3	1978	c 27'
Symphony No. 9 op.128	D major	4	1986	c 52'

*Scherzo develops from and is part of first movement.
+Scherzo episode in middle movement.
†Established only in the last movement.

Nine are numbered, which begs the question - why didn't the composer include (as some other symphonic composers have[3]) works for smaller

[1] Sir Malcolm Arnold (1921 – 2006) *I think about music in terms of sound - The Guardian,* 3 June 1971.
[2] The are also three *Sinfoniettas* and a *Symphonic Suite for Orchestra, op. 12.*
[3] Honegger, Shostakovich, Miaskovsky, William Schuman, Roy Harris, etc.

forces in the numbered cycle? My guess is that Arnold felt that a Symphony for Strings as a 'First Symphony' would go unnoticed. Having set that precedent, he excluded the Symphony for Brass. It would have been entertaining had he numbered all twelve and therefore included the Toy Symphony! There is also the question of the time-scale of the symphonic canvass. The unnumbered symphonies are shorter works. The average Arnold symphony lasts around 30' plus or minus five minutes.[4] The exceptions are numbers 7 and 9, of which the latter is the longest in the cycle by a considerable margin. On the evidence of the work itself and the composer's comments on it (see below), Arnold shared – with Bruckner, Mahler and others – the notion that after Beethoven, a 'Ninth' should be, in scale and content, a summation of achievement. It is also interesting to note that the pattern of longer and shorter works in the numbered cycle – aside from the Sixth – follows the pattern of Beethoven's cycle. However, it is probably a coincidence.

2 The 'classical' symphonist

At first glance, Arnold's symphonic cycle might be defined as abstract music on a classical/early romantic canvas. Arnold was not interested in the line of development in post-Beethovenian symphonic music that led to the hybrid symphony (programmatic – vocal – symphonic poem etc.). All twelve symphonies are either in three or in four movements. Each Symphony has a home key.[5] In comparison with his great British contemporary Robert Simpson (1921 – 1997), Arnold's approach to abstract form is less radical, but within the boundaries in which Arnold worked, his handling of form is imaginative, subtle and often original.

As we approach the questions of 'extraneous' musical elements (see below), it is tempting to draw a parallel between Arnold and the Eighteenth Century symphonic tradition in general, and Haydn in particular. There are,

---

[4] These timings are taken (averaged) from the three complete recordings currently available but it is interesting to note that Arnold's recording of Symphony No 4 (Lyrita) lasts a massive 54' 13'' - all the more surprising given that the sketches for Symphony No 8 start with precise timing (in seconds) for sections of yet-to-be-written music, which match the metronome markings. Perhaps the explanation for this is that Arnold's experience as a film composer led him to think in precise timings but Arnold as a conductor interpreted the music as he felt it during the performance.

[5] But see Symphony for Brass (below)

after all, military marches and allusions to 'ethnic' styles in symphonic music of the Classical period. Such an analogy would be a neat explanation and legitimise Arnold as an abstract symphonic composer whilst separating him from the later 'purist' symphonic tradition of Sibelius, Simpson and others. It doesn't fit because of the high profile that these elements assume, both structurally and stylistically.

3 Orchestral forces

The scale of the symphonic canvass is mirrored in the orchestral forces used. In this respect the model may have been Sibelius who used the larger 'Romantic' orchestra in some of the tone poems, but in the symphonies, wrote for the same forces that Brahms had used, with few 'extras'. Arnold's basic line-up in the numbered symphonies is:

- Woodwind: 2 2 2 2 with some doublings and a maximum of two additional players;
- Brass: 4 3 3 1;
- Timpani (maximum of three, sometimes with set tunings)
- Strings

Plus

- Harp and celesta in most works;
- Percussion[6] – sometimes a large array of instruments but a maximum of three players (normally two)

Although this line-up is a link to the Brahms/Sibelius conception of symphonic orchestral forces, it should be noted that it is common to most of Arnold's orchestral output. He saw no need for the late-romantic orchestra and disliked certain timbres (such as the cor anglais). Arnold did not need the massive forces of a Mahlerian orchestra to create a multi-dimensional sound-world.

---

[6] Except in Symphony No 3.

4 Use of forms

Arnold used traditional forms such as sonata, variation, rondo and fugue/fugato. The handling of sonata form in particular becomes more subtle and elusive in the later works. Traditional forms are seldom, if ever, used merely as a template to be filled with musical ideas but they do serve as a point of contact with the listener, allowing the composer to play with the listener's expectations.

Time signatures normally remain unchanged for an entire movement. Notable exceptions are the adjoined Scherzo in No 3, the scherzo episode in the slow middle movement of no 6, the 'Irish' episode in the finale of No 7, and the quick central section of the first movement of the Symphony for Brass. Without recourse to frequent time signature changes,[7] Arnold, generates powerful rhythmic structures (including widespread use of ostinato rhythms) and a high level of rhythmic interest.

5 The musical journey

To a greater or lesser extent, a sense of unity is achieved through subtle motific connections across movements (these are discussed in detail below). Only in the Fifth Symphony does Arnold directly quote and develop material across movements, and to overwhelming effect, making it the most concentrated and unified in the cycle. In some works, notably the Third and Sixth, the emotional currents of the previous movements seem to be abandoned in the finale. In others, notably the First and Fourth Symphonies, Arnold delivers shock endings that seem to derail the emotional logic of the work at the final hurdle. The Fifth also has a shock ending but one that stems from the logic of the whole work and is therefore more satisfying. The major key endings of all but two of the symphonies (Symphony for Strings and Symphony No 5) often carry a sense of irony.

6 Treatment of tonality

The music of Malcolm Arnold is tonal in so far as each work in the numbered cycle has a home key. Tonal relationships between movements

---

[7] A single 3/8 bar in the middle movement of the Symphony for Strings, and a 3/4 bar that comes twice in the first movement of No 8 are odd exceptions.

are often unconventional in comparison to Eighteenth and Nineteenth-century models. In particular, Arnold favours key centres for middle movements that are a tone or semitone above or below the main key. Arnold's musical language embraces simple functional tonality, more complex tonal writing, modal writing, bitonality and (later in the cycle) serialism. In the Fifth and Eighth symphonies, Arnold constructs layers of tonal/non-tonal writing that work against each other.

7 Thematic material

Arnold's thematic material includes:

- Self-contained tonal themes; which appear as 'musical objects' and are not developed;
- Open-ended themes – which have strong antecedents but weaker consequents that need to be fulfilled through their structural context (for instance, the opening theme of Symphony No. 2);
- Fragments: themes that are cut short (see Symphonies No. 1 and No. 3 below);
- Motifs;
- Ciphers (pitch material in which names are encrypted) and other symbolic pitch formations;
- Tone rows.

8 Definable extra-musical elements

Arnold's programme notes have a light touch and can even be misleading. But we know that an element of Symphony No. 4 is an expression of Arnold's feeling of solidarity with ethnic minorities. The Fifth Symphony is, in part, a memorial to four recently departed friends. Symphony No. 7 is dedicated to Arnold's three children; each child is the focus of a particular movement, but beyond that, the programmatic/descriptive elements of each movement, though vividly represented in the musical discourse and through musical symbols, is neither explained by the composer, nor 'guessable' by the listener.

9 Indefinable extra-musical elements

I have a number of strong beliefs which are the basis of all my work. If anyone listens without prejudice to all my music, he will be able to see clearly what these beliefs are...[8]

It is not clear from this statement whether Arnold is referring to his position in relation to compositional technique and the music of his time (about which he had a great deal to say) or something extra-musical. If it is the latter, the present writer must declare that he is *unable* to see clearly what those beliefs are. This brings me to the vexed question of Arnold's 'musical symbols', by which I mean sounds, extraneous stylistic elements and processes that have undisclosed significance and often stand outside the context of the abstract musical logic of a work. These include:

- Funeral Marches
- Military Marches
- Military symbolism (such as fanfares and funereal 'last post' brass solos etc.)
- Ethnic elements (Caribbean and Irish)
- Popular styles (jazz, popular/light, cinematic)
- Sonorities (for example, the large cowbell that closes each movement of Symphony no 7 and is, according to Arnold, "a symbol of hope" - and the use of Bartokian 'Night Music' effects)

10 Stylistic influences

Arnold lists Sibelius and Mahler as his two favourite composers, with the reservation that Mahler is less of a model because "*the unity of the form is often difficult to grasp*".[9] Although there is not a single bar in the cycle that could have been written by anyone but Arnold, both Sibelius and Mahler left an imprint on his style. The influence of Sibelius is more apparent in the earlier Symphonies; the Mahlerian influences in the later ones, particularly Symphonies Five, Seven and Nine. I would go as far as to suggest that we are *supposed* to recall the *Adagietto* from Mahler's Fifth when we hear the opening of the slow movement of Arnold's Fifth. Other

---

[8] Sir Malcolm Arnold (1921 – 2006) *I think about music in terms of sound - The Guardian* 3 June 1971
[9] Ibid

influences include Berlioz, Bartok (in the 'night music' passages), Nielsen and Shostakovich. The notion of Arnold as an 'English Shostakovich' has recently gained momentum. What are the parallels? Stylistic similarities certainly, but more broadly, the sense of a musical subtext behind the notes. Passages of violence and brutality, child-like simplicity, irony and banality occur in the symphonic cycles of both composers. However, Shostakovich composed in a climate of fear and under censorship. Arnold was free to write whatever he pleased. He did not pander to the critics, though he eventually paid the price in terms of reputation and high-profile performances.

The name of Nielsen does not appear in the major studies of Arnold's music. Yet I find that the direction in which Arnold travelled has something in common with the last two of Nielsen's six Symphonies, especially the Fifth, which he obviously knew and was directly influenced by.[10] That said, it is impossible to align Arnold directly with any particular symphonic school or aesthetic, or to go very far beyond the composer's own cryptic statements quoted above.

Analytical Commentaries:

A dry run: Symphony for Strings Op. 13 (1946)

Malcolm Arnold's first wife, Sheila (*nee* Nicholson), was a member of the London-based Riddick String Orchestra. This connection led to the commission for Arnold's first work that bears the title 'Symphony'. It was first performed in April 1947.

Anyone hearing the Symphony for Strings without knowing in advance the name of the composer might be surprised to discover that it is by Arnold. It is a concise but powerful three-movement work and, along with the Fifth, the only Symphony that begins and ends in a minor key. It is also, apart from the Toy Symphony, op. 62, the only Symphony by Arnold that displays unanimity of style and mood throughout, which in this case is astringent in tone and has a prevailingly dark mood. The high seriousness of the work is evident in Arnold's suppression of his outstanding melodic gifts, which is not to say that the work is unmemorable, merely un-

[10] See Symphony No 1 below

ingratiating. The intricate working of small motifs, especially in the first movement, and the *salterello* dance-style of the finale, point towards the First Symphony.

Symphonic debut: Symphony No 1 Op. 22 (1948/9)

Malcolm Arnold completed his First Symphony on 16 February 1949. It was not commissioned. The work was taken up by the Cheltenham Festival and premiered in Cheltenham Town Hall on 6 July 1951 under the composer's baton. It lasts just under half an hour and is in the key of D (initially D minor[11]). The work is bold, original and concentrated. The first movement, marked *Allegro,* opens with one of Arnold's most arresting ideas:

Ex. 1a

It consists of just three pitches (F – G – (F) – D) naggingly repeated and hammered into different shapes that create cross-rhythms. The key is undefined until bar 6, when the woodwind enter above a tonic (D) pedal. The tonality veers away from D minor (Dorian), shifting towards Eb minor. At fig. **B,** Arnold sets up a marching bass accompaniment:

Ex. 1b

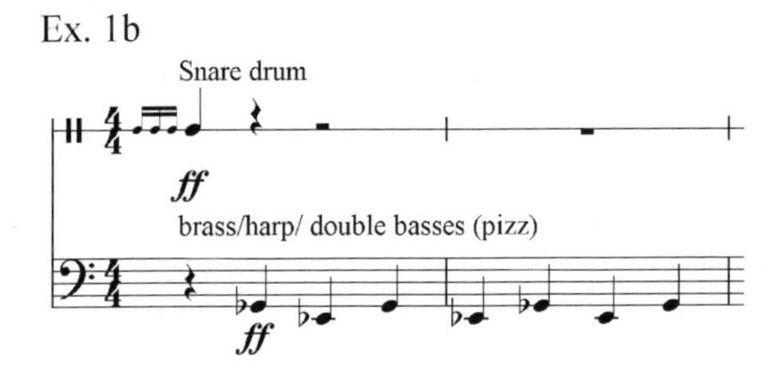

[11] The evidence that Arnold thought of the whole Symphony as a minor key work is outlined below (see Symphony No 5).

This, in combination with the shrill high-woodwind ostinati, accompanies a lengthy dialogue between horns, trumpets and strings. The war-like gestures in general and the figuration in particular, strongly suggest the influence of Nielsen's Fifth Symphony (first section), a work that Arnold must surely have known.[12] Via a series of slow harmonic shifts, encased in soaring string arpeggios and trumpet fanfares, the tonality edges back towards the home key – D minor. A quiet transition based on Ex. 1a leads to a new tempo *poco meno mosso.* Echoes of Ex.1a & Ex.1b punctuate the entries of the short phrase that serves as the second subject. It is in the relative major (F major) and played by muted strings, echoed by the harp:

Ex. 1c

Ex. 1c is a fragment that seems in need of completion but never achieves it either here or in its reprise.[13] In this long F major section we hear the fragment many times, with subtle variations, including a switch from Bb to B natural, invokes the Aeolian/Dorian ambiguity at the start of the movement. Ex. 1a hovers in the background throughout this passage. Thus far Arnold has created a sense of expansiveness via the slow pace of key change and continual working of small motifs. Here, (as in some of the later symphonies), Arnold moves swiftly onwards to conclude the movement in a development/recapitulation of roughly the same length as the exposition. The formal unveiling of themes over a large stretch of time does not need to be repeated for the sake of convention. It has served to familiarise the listener with the material ahead of a compressed development/recapitulation that racks up the tension. In his approach to form, Arnold may have learned lessons from the first movement of Sibelius' Fourth Symphony, a work which Arnold regarded as *"The greatest work of modern times"*.[14]. Of particular fascination is the brief

[12] The Peterloo Overture (1967) contains a passage of solo snare drum writing almost identical to the snare drum solo in Nielsen's Fifth.

[13] The second subject of the first movement of Symphony No. 3 is also presented as a fragment (see below).

[14] Interview with R.M. Schafer: *British Composers in Interview,* Faber and Faber.

reappearance of the second subject (Ex. 1c) set against a strange Bartokian texture of wind and harp tremulandi, trills and string (later trombone) glissandi. The simple key-conflict (D – Eb minor – F Lydian) of the exposition is widened, setting up powerful tensions that continue through to the final bars. Arnold's highly selective recall of fragments from the exposition is enough to clinch the form, and the added sixth – D minor (Dorian) chord of the final bars wrenches the music away from Eb minor to bring the movement to an abrupt but convincing close.

The second movement, marked *Andantino* is in C major. It is a long movement, almost entirely quiet and characterised by strange Bartokian sounds such as ostinati based on string glissandi, exposed (sometimes accented) harp notes and eerie solos for brass. Unusually, Arnold uses only one theme. Ex. 1d is a theme of gentle intimacy, its character captured in the scoring (violins, then solo flute):

Ex. 1d

The accompaniment uses subtle imitation whilst sustaining the key chord above a pedal E. Throughout the opening paragraph the static C major chord nudges towards, but doesn't reach root-position. Arnold's control of register and long-range harmonic structure is a model of tonal prolongation, in which fleeting resolutions to a C major 5/3 chord only appear in the middle register until the final bars, to create the effect of a full resolution. E is therefore treated as a pedal point. Arnold highlights this in many places by means of sudden short pauses followed by accented Es. At fig. **D** the low pedal becomes an ostinato figure:

Ex. 1e

Thus far the pitch content of the movement has been strictly diatonic. At fig. E, a swaying F/E becomes F#/E, subtly linking the figure to the rising and falling major seconds of the first movement's main motif (Ex. 1a). This provokes a sudden *fortissimo* outburst (woodwind/brass) on triads a tritone apart (E minor/Bb minor). The two chords are played off against each other, initially in small fragmentary exchanges, then as a three-part dialogue based on Ex. 1d. The Bb minor triad shifts down to A major, softening the dissonance and preparing for a full recapitulation but with the main events in reverse order. The long-awaited resolution to a root-position C major chord is intensely satisfying, and is achieved by re-establishing the pedal E and descending by step down to the root – C. The image of lovers on the verge of sleep, listening to the sounds of the night before sleep envelops them, is hard to resist as one hears this tender and mysterious movement.

The finale is marked *Vivace con fuoco.* Here Arnold engages with a long tradition amongst British symphonists[15] of writing fugal finales (complete fugues or, more commonly, structures crowned by a fugato episode). If the intention (Arnold's and others) is to honour the Everest of musical forms with the ultimate academic challenge, Arnold's must surely be the most bizarre. Early commentators felt that Arnold did not (even *could* not) 'follow the rules'. Yet he does, and the seamless flow from subject to counter-subject, not to mention the assured handling of a regular exposition that grows to four-part texture, is evidence of the composer's technical virtuosity. The subject is *saltarello*-like (perhaps a memory of Arnold's recent compositional sojourn to Italy, as commentators have suggested), full of vigour and built to generate rhythmic energy and harmonic tension:

[15] Elgar, Vaughan Williams , Walton, Tippett, Bliss and others

Ex. 1f

As is usual in a sonata-fugue, the fugal sections alternate with short 'free-textured' developmental episodes, used to create many transformations of the material. The first counter-exposition, at letter **J,** is lightly scored for solo woodwinds, and runs to three entries over a pedal point. The second, at letter **U**, is quieter still (***pp***) and scored for strings. Here there are four entries, with subject and counter-subject in inversion. The shortest but most dramatic is at letter **DD**; a full-orchestral multi-layered stretto. It comes to an abrupt halt when, for no apparent reason, a G major fanfare heralds the first of two bizarre transformations of the subject. It is a military march (marked *Alla Marcia*) in C major, (the key of the slow movement and also the logical choice to harmonise the subject in simple tonality but at the original pitch) led by two piccolos and a flute above a marching bass, a trumpet adding the rhythmic character of a military fanfare at the second statement; horns blaring the theme against full orchestra at the final *tutti* statement:

Ex 1g

The second transformation of Ex. 1f,,in 3/2 time and marked *Maestoso,* is processional in character and set above a three note ostinato (the first three notes of the subject in double augmentation). As Hugo Cole has pointed out[16], it is reminiscent of the final peroration of Stravinsky's *Symphony of Psalms* (1930, rev.1948). Another probable influence – represented by the pulse, tempo, texture and, particularly, the repeated accented dominant octaves five bars before the end, may have been the coda of Sibelius' Fifth

---

[16] Hugo Cole: Malcolm Arnold: An Introduction to his Music.

Symphony. For some commentators, the final episode seems out of proportion to the length of the movement (indeed the whole Symphony) and therefore overblown. However, after the absurdity of the little march, it restores some measure of seriousness and harmonic intensity.

Why does the First Symphony end in such an unexpected way and what message, if any, are we given? Was the composer simply delighted that his material had the scope for such transformation and couldn't resist the temptation to do it? Anthony Meredith and Paul Harris[17] propose a fascinating interpretation of the work in light of Arnold's wartime experiences and pacifist beliefs. Military symbolism returns later in the cycle, at the same point in the finale of the Fourth, and with more sinister effect in the finale of the Fifth and the first movement of the Eighth. The coda of Arnold's First Symphony announces the composer's willingness to turn expectations on their head at the last moment and deliver an outcome that was unforeseeable at any point in the work.

A sunny day: Symphony No 2 Op. 40 (1953)

Arnold's Second Symphony followed swiftly on the heels of the premiere of the First. When the newly appointed Principal conductor of the Bournemouth Municipal Orchestra, Charles Groves, contacted the composer to enquire about a commission, Arnold offered the new symphony that he was writing. He completed it in February 1953. The first performance took place on 25 May 1953. The critical reception was the most positive that the composer ever received for a symphonic work. Symphony No 2 travelled widely, helping to establish Arnold's international reputation. It ranks jointly with the Fifth as the most frequently recorded symphony (six recordings to date) in the cycle. It is easy to understand why. Though arguably less profound than the later symphonies, Symphony No 2 embraces a wide emotional range and is thoroughly engaging. It is rightly regarded by commentators as a work that is close to perfection.

The home key is Eb major. The opening movement is the least dramatic first movement in the cycle, and suggests that the work will be lightweight. Arnold likened it to "a sunny day". It is fast-moving and concise. As in the

---

[17] *Malcolm Arnold; Rogue Genius* Thames /Elkin

First Symphony, the handling of sonata form is not formulaic. The exposition lays out the themes on a broad canvass. The development and recapitulation are compacted to raise the level of drama. Arnold follows convention in the exposition, except for placing the second subject in the most distant key – A major – rather than in the dominant. The three main statements – first subject, transition theme, second subject – are all lyrical in character but their roles in the structure are clearly defined. The first theme (Ex. 2a) is open-ended; the transition (Ex. 2b) is tonally unstable: the second subject (Ex. 2c) warmer than the first and tonally/harmonically self-contained:

The first theme highlights the interval of a perfect fourth, which is associated with tonal stability within the movement[18], and connects the main themes of the work. Arnold uses thirds (Ex. 2b) to highlight passages that are transitional and tonally unstable. A two bar introductory figure also highlights the fourth, leaving Ex. 2a to confirm the key. We hear Ex. 2a three times in succession. Each restatement is more warmly scored and embellished texturally and harmonically. Ex. 2b (scored for woodwind) immediately dissolves the home key and introduces a higher norm of dissonance. A sudden restoration of key via a II6 – V 6/4 – 5/3 (tinged with tongue-in-cheek sentimentality) precedes Ex. 2c, which is heard twice (woodwind, then lower strings). Note the use of chromatic slides – one of Arnold's fingerprints, and redolent of popular styles. Much of the brief development is based on fragments that were incidental in the exposition but now assume greater importance. Out of this process, a significant scalic motif emerges:

Ex. 2d

Arnold allows space for a full statement of Ex. 2a in the remote key of C major. The listener does not need to have perfect pitch to know that this is not yet the start of the recapitulation. Unusual though it is to quote the whole theme at this point in the movement, the complex accompaniment – a combination of a shimmering string texture, strands of the theme in augmentation, and the semiquaver motif (Ex. 2d) – signal the structural context. Up until the start of the recapitulation the music has been lightly scored and quiet. Arnold steers the music to the home key and delivers a masterstroke. The first and second subjects (Ex. 2a and Ex. 2c) flow into a single expanse of melody without the transition theme (which appears after this episode), and with Ex. 2d played by the woodwind (the effect is reminiscent of the closing pages of Sibelius' Second Symphony). It makes a thrilling climax. Had the movement ended here it would have sounded

[18] The intervallic structure of the first bar happens to echo Ex. 1f (Symphony No. 1).

abrupt. A sudden change of dynamic precedes the last appearance of Ex. 2a, scored, as on its first appearance, for solo clarinet. Arnold then revisits the transition theme (Ex. 2b), thereby briefly destabilising the key to make the final page (a thinly scored *fortissimo* after a swift crescendo from ***pp***) a satisfying resolution, complete with the 'fourth' motif (Bb/Eb) hammered out by the timpani. Within the space of a mere six minutes, all musical issues have been resolved.

The second movement, *Vivace* is a 6/8 scherzo, Arnold's first in a Symphony but in a line of succession from the brilliant overture *Beckus the Dandipratt* op. 5 (1943). The form is loosely A–B–A. The second 'A' section is a compact and climactic variation of the first 'A' section. The central 'B' section is woven into the movement without the need for a break in continuity to signal the event. Though mainly scored for strings (muted and *spiccato*), the 'B' section echoes Ex. 2b (first movement) by virtue of its contrary motion thirds, soft dynamics and tonal instability. Commentators have noted the Sibelian influence here, and the composer himself acknowledged it. The model may have been the gossamer 12/8 section in *Tapiola, op. 112* which it closely resembles. Other echoes of *Tapiola* include the rushing woodwind scales that first appear in bar 6.

The main body of the Scherzo is a network of small motifs and fleeting harmonic fragments. The key centre is G major/minor but it is only hinted at, kept in reserve until the appearance of the roguish main theme:

Ex. 2e

Initially Ex. 2e is lightly scored. It appears in different guises, making its final appearance – a spectacular *fortissimo* tutti (unharmonised) – a bracing climax to a movement which is spectral and picaresque in character. Aside from the prominent rising fourth motif in Ex. 2e that links their opening themes, the first two movements are strikingly different. By making the Scherzo darker and more powerful than the first movement, Arnold announces that the Symphony is a weightier and more complex a work than the listener first imagined.

The third movement is marked *Lento*. It is sustained, subdued and elegiac, culminating in the presentation of the main theme as a funeral march, which confirms the key centre, B minor. Commentators have noted the influence of Mahler, drawing parallels between this march and the one that appears in Mahler's First Symphony. It may well have been a direct influence, but the mood is Arnold's; sombre, though without the harrowing emotionalism and parody of the later symphonic marches.[19]

The main theme is passed from the bassoon (in the high register) to the violas and finally to the oboe; each choice of timbre exemplifying the mood:

Ex. 2f

Despite the repetitions of this long theme, Arnold holds the listener's attention by means of subtle changes of figuration, rhythm and expression. There are many short developmental episodes during the movement. A second element, essentially harmonic and rhythmic, grows out of the accompaniment to Ex. 2f on its second appearance and quickly develops as a separate motif:

Ex. 2g

The thirds-based chord construction, a link to episodes in the first and second movements, generates this motif, repeatedly exclaimed by shrill woodwinds:

---

[19] See commentary on Symphony No. 6 - in which the slow movement follows the same sequence of events.

Ex. 2h

After the funeral march episode the ostinato accompaniment (Ex. 2i) abates for a brief recapitulation of the main theme (this time given to solo horn) but re-enters in the final four bars, leaving no doubt as to the underlying character of the movement.

Ex. 2i

The finale, marked *Allegro con brio,* is launched with a blaze of rhythmicised Eb major tonic chords. Timpani emphasise the tonic/dominant fourths motif that runs through the whole work, and supports the main theme of the finale in augmentation:

Ex. 2j

The breezy tune is given a humorous touch by turning the final bar of its two phrases from 2/4 to 6/8 by adding a waltz rhythm in lower brass in the extended bars. The key changes abruptly to E minor. Arnold launches a bold theme, in E minor, on unison horns, punctuated by staccato tonic chords scored for full orchestra:

Ex. 2k

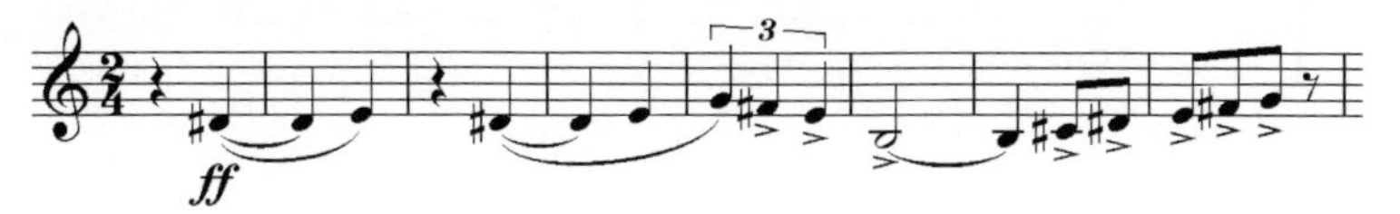

It enters four times, building to four-part imitative texture. Some commentators describe the passage as a fugue. Fugato might be a more appropriate term. Moreover, the sequence is Subject – Subject – Answer – Subject, so we hear, initially, a canonic process. The two main themes are repeated without transition, and rescored. In the case of the second theme, the quiet scoring and displacement of rhythmic accents transforms its character almost beyond recognition. The care and ingenuity with which Arnold satisfies the need for restatement within a symphonic structure, but avoids simple repetition, is a hallmark of the composer's style.

A quiet development section based on the first theme interweaves a network of fragments many of which recall figuration from the first and second movements. The music settles on a pedal E. We hear the second theme one last time; the high solo bassoon scoring recreating the sound-world of the start of the preceding *Lento* movement. The main rondo theme has its final airing, beginning quietly and building to a tutti ahead of the grand coda. It is marked *Lento molto e maestoso* and is in 4/4 time. If one shares the view that the slow 'processional' endings of Arnold's early symphonies are overblown, this one is well proportioned in relation to the finale and the Symphony as a whole. A quiet, throw-away ending would perhaps have been a braver choice, but Arnold makes a vital structural point by hammering out the opening of the rondo theme and showing us that the rising fourth is the kernel of the Symphony's thematic argument. The opening notes of the fugato theme reappear as chromatic appoggiaturas that resolve into the harmony and prolong the tension.

Arnold's Second Symphony is the most approachable of the Nine but should not be undervalued for that reason. If the First Symphony represents a young composer's 'declaration of intent' as a serious symphonist, it cleared the air for a Second Symphony that allowed Arnold to display the full range of his style (up to that point) in a single work and call it, with justification, a Symphony.

Child's play: Toy Symphony Op. 62 (1957)

Mention must be made of Arnold's magnificent Toy Symphony, which was written in aid of the Musician's Benevolent Fund and composed in the same year as the Third Symphony.

A detailed analysis of the work would be contrary to the spirit of this touching comic masterpiece. Instead, I'll confine myself to a few observations:

1. It is the shortest of the symphonies
2. It is the only Symphony by Arnold scored for unconventional forces (Quail, Cuckoo + Guard's Whistle, Whistle in C# minor + Nightingale, three toy trumpets, three dulcimers, Triangle, Cymbal, Drum, String Quartet (or string orchestra), Piano);
3. The title is a link to the Classical era;
4. The first movement is another example of Arnold's love of march rhythms and military symbolism;
5. The finale, like that of the Symphony for Strings and Symphony No 1, is a *salterello* –like dance movement;
6. All three movements follow simple clear-cut musical forms;
7. The key of the central movement maintains Arnold's preference for keys one degree either side of the tonic (E minor in a work in F major).

Highs and lows: Symphony No. 3, Op. 63 (1957)

When William Walton indicated that his Second Symphony would not be ready on time for the scheduled première, the Royal Liverpool Philharmonic Society turned to Malcolm Arnold and commissioned a new Symphony from him. Arnold dedicated the work to the Royal Liverpool Philharmonic Society. The first performance took place on 2 December 1957 at the Royal Festival Hall, conducted by John Pritchard. Circumstances suggest that the work was written at high speed. It was probably begun immediately after completing the Scottish Dances (1957), though some commentators suggest a longer gestation. If it was written at high speed, there are no signs of haste in the work, which is on a larger scale than its predecessors.

Arnold's Third Symphony is in many respects an austere work. Arnold denies himself the colouristic resources of harp, celesta and percussion (except for timpani). There are no sudden changes of style or extraneous musical influences. The first two movements are on a larger scale than anything that came before, though as in the Seventh Symphony, the finale is more classically proportioned.

In this symphony Arnold inhabits two opposing emotional worlds – tragedy and joy. The juxtaposition of the two has confounded some commentators, yet there are plenty of precedents (most obviously Beethoven and Mahler). The formal scheme of the work, in which the central movement is placed in the remotest key from the home key (Bb major) and the first two movements contain tonal instability within large-scale formal structures, is illustrated below:

First Movement *Allegro - Vivace*	**Second Movement** *Lento*	**Third Movement** *Allegro con brio*
Bb major	E minor	Bb major
Emotionally complex, with sudden changes of mood.	Tragic	Joyous
Tonally unstable; passages based on chord changes every one or two bars; two brief periods of tonal stability associated with the second subject (in F major (dominant) and later Bb major (tonic)).	Theme (8 bars) – twenty variations (sometimes extended by one or two bars) – coda. Chord changes in each bar but the home key (E minor) is reiterated at the start of each variation. The climactic coda (8 bars) is built entirely on the tonic chord.	Tonal stability and a clear 'classical' formal structure.

Of the first movement, Arnold gave this description:

The first movement has two main subjects, the first of which is played by the violins, violas, flutes and bassoon at the very outset of the piece. Later on, the second subject is first stated by the oboe accompanied by the violins. Towards the end of the movement the tempo abruptly changes and the material is developed as a scherzo.[20]

The fusion of sonata allegro and scherzo into a single movement has one obvious precedent, which Arnold acknowledged – the opening movement of Sibelius' Fifth Symphony. However, the two are so different that it is clear that the Sibelius was merely a point of departure, not a model. The bulk of Arnold's movement is the main *Allegro*; the 6/8 *Vivace* acts as a postscript, marking a point of high drama at its start, then winding down to a sudden quiet close. A stronger influence may have been Sibelius' Fourth Symphony in which the sonata first movement and the scherzo are separated by a pause, but thematically connected[21]. Sibelius' scherzo ends quietly and abruptly, as does Arnold's.

The formal plan is broadly

- Section 1 (Exposition, with developmental passages);
- Section 2 (Second (shorter) exposition, with further development of the material);
- Section 3 (one new thematic element plus a short recapitulation of the principal themes transformed into a scherzo).

In his programme note, Arnold describes the opening as the first subject. He may well have written it first and not derived it from Ex. 3b, but hearing the two in sequence, Ex. 3a sounds like the outline of a theme yet to be stated:

[20] Arnold's programme note

[21] As were the first and second movements of Sibelius' Fifth in the first (1915) version, although Arnold would not have known the first version at the time of writing his work (it was made available for a one-off recording in 1996).

Ex. 3a

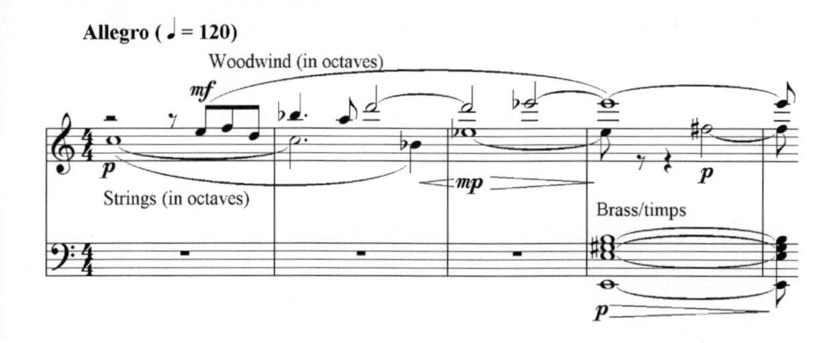

The mood is calm and expectant. The string theme undermines the woodwind theme by anticipating the resolution of the harmony, and the sense of key is further undermined by the arrival of a remote E major seventh chord. The gesture is repeated, shifting closer to the home key.

The main theme is introduced by cellos and violas:

Ex. 3b

The melody, with accompaniment texture and regular phrase structure, signal the arrival of the definitive theme. However, the tonality is unstable throughout, and at this point in the movement the pattern of harmonic changes in one-bar (later two-bar) periods is established. Launched in D minor (reiterated in G minor), it evades the home key. There are four statements of the theme. After the first two, Arnold launches a brief development marked by brass fanfare rhythms and veering towards the home key. A new figure appears:

Ex. 3c

The material contains the seed of the second subject. There is a striking similarity of texture, mood and gesture between this passage and passages in the first and third movements of Sibelius' Sixth Symphony. Also, it shares with the transition theme of Arnold's Second Symphony the use of parallel thirds and rapid key changes. Arnold's scoring is buoyant to the point of comic effect – tuba and flute adding to the character of the passage. With the return of Ex. 3b the mood darkens. The theme is more lightly scored, with a persistent low E on the timpani:

Ex. 3d

solo

mp

It acts as a leading note to the entry of the second subject in the dominant key (F major/Lydian):

Ex. 3e

The wistful opening breaks off abruptly at the falling fourth, which is used to 'heckle' the phrase whenever it appears. This process continues, with increasing violence at each statement of the theme. At fig. **H** the 'heckling' figure takes off as an independent episode. Horns and then trumpets attempt to break through the fractured texture with a full statement of Ex. 3e but the passage is abruptly silenced by the timpani (Ex. 3d).

Although section 1 announces and repeats each theme in turn, there is much small-scale development and use of thematic cross-reference along the way. This also happens in section 2, which is launched by a minor key variant of Ex. 3c, followed by small developmental passages from section 1, again, differently harmonised, leaving room only for a full restatement of the first subject before a powerful collision between Ex. 3a in stretto and the 'heckling' motif.

The brief transition to section 3 (scherzo) reiterates the harmonic progression of the first four bars (Ex. 3a), paving the way for the only new motif that belongs to the scherzo (though it can be heard as an intervallic expansion of the 'heckling' motif):

Ex. 3f

Much of the brief scherzo is an interaction between Ex. 3f and Exs. 3a/b, the latter reconfigured in 6/8 time. At one point, Arnold retraces the harmonic steps of Ex. 3b, replacing the theme with Ex. 3f. There is no *grand dénouement*. In the closing pages of the movement, the orchestration thins out. The second subject (Ex. 3d, played by solo flute, with little alteration) closes the movement. It marks the return to the home key (Bb major/Lydian) and creates a brief plateaux of harmonic stability. Only the key is resolved. The sudden change of mood after such a combative scherzo, and the brevity of the reprise, leaves the emotional agenda on hold. Taken as a whole, the first movement is a gripping voyage built on instantly memorable themes and fragments. In music that is often dark and disturbing there are kaleidoscopic changes of mood. Subtly integrated through close motific connections, with clear structural signposts throughout its span, the music sits on a bedrock of constantly shifting key centres and a relentless succession of changing chords.

In some respects the second movement is easier for the listener to navigate. Arnold describes it as

Elegiac in character...a set of variations on a series of chords more than a melodic theme.

The movement is in the remote key of E minor (i.e. the furthest distance from the home key, Bb). There are twenty variations (one slightly extended) on the eight-bar theme, and a short coda (letter **V**), marked *fortissimo,* which is purely harmonic – a reiterated E minor chord.

Ex. 3g

Though much of the movement is quiet and sparingly scored, the climaxes have a shattering effect and the ending dispels any doubt as to the tragic nature of the movement. The underlying chords of the theme are the main substance of the movement, along with small motifs from Ex. 3g that are reassembled into fresh themes. The dominant figure – which pervades all of the climaxes – is the tail motif ('x') of the Theme. It is used in augmentation and diminution. Significant new rhythmic elements appear and reappear in the course the movement, of which this timpani rhythm lends a funereal character:

Ex. 3h

It is interesting to compare the movement with Britten's Passacaglia from the opera *Peter Grimes*. The mood is similar, and Arnold's tail motif (X) is close to being an inversion of the main motif that underpins Britten's Interlude. The difference is that Britten creates a trajectory of rising tension and drama towards a single overwhelming climax. The climactic moments in Arnold's movement are shattering but they do not arise through a discernable emotional narrative. The listener is locked into a claustrophobic world of pain in which time stands still.

In his programme note, Arnold states that the last movement is

based on three main themes and could loosely be described as a rondo.

The breezy first theme is cunningly outlined in an introduction that reminds us of the 'heckling' motif from the first movement. The home key – Bb major – is quickly established and some momentary sidesteps are immediately called into check. The fourths motif is embedded in the theme itself, whose opening is loosely reminiscent of guitar tuning. The continuation is extended via an ornamental figure before retracing its steps. Note the palindromic shape (strict palindromes become important in the later symphonies) and the sudden change of tonal orientation at the end:

Ex. 3i

The theme – one of Arnold's most attractive symphonic inspirations – seems to banish the conflict of the previous movements. We hear an augmented version of Ex. 3i which extends the theme further. Another reminder of the 'heckling' passage is swept aside by the entry of the second theme:

Ex. 3j

Built on simple triadic figures and therefore harmonically unambiguous, it is scored for unison violins, violas and cellos and is lightly accompanied. A louder reiteration of the theme is supported by a resplendent C major #13th chord. The two themes are played again (the first in its lyrical augmented version) but presented in new guises. There is a brief developmental episode which moves away from the tonic. Ex. 3i reappears at figure **F**. What follows is a more extended development episode – a brilliant interplay of fragments and shifting tonal perspectives. There is a strange moment of stasis built upon repeated chords a tritone apart (the central episode of the finale of Sibelius' Fourth Symphony may have been an influence). Tonal stability is soon re-established and the home key is in sight. At letter **K** Arnold introduces the third theme, built on rising and falling seventh chords:

Ex. 3k

The preceding themes appear once more before the tempo increases to *Presto* at the start of the coda. Over a long rhythmically charged dominant pedal, Arnold melts the harmonic tensions of the movement and, with one last statement of motif 'y' from Ex 3i, ends the movement on a tonic chord embellished with rippling fanfares.

Some commentators have described the ending of Arnold's Third Symphony as "overblown". I disagree. Just as the ending of the second movement is unambiguously tragic, the ending of the finale presents an unstoppable wave of joyfulness that grows directly from the musical argument of the finale *as a whole*: something that we do not encounter again in an Arnold symphony. There is no hint of irony here. The stability of the home key supports the mood of the movement as a whole and counters the instability of the preceding movements. We are left feeling that the Symphony is an essentially positive and uplifting work, even if the memory pain cannot be completely banished. Whether or not one empathises with Arnold's vision, it is unarguably truthful and highly personal.

A man of his times: Symphony No 4 Op. 71 (1960)

Malcolm Arnold's Fourth Symphony was commissioned by the BBC, completed in July 1960 and premiered on 2nd November 1960 by the BBC Symphony Orchestra, conducted by the composer.

The work is in four movements. The home key is F *Lydian* – a point that Arnold drew attention to in his programme note. The composer also pointed out that the orchestra is a *standard* orchestra (not a large one, as some commentators describe it). The line-up is the same as that used in the Second Symphony but with the addition of celesta and one more percussionist. It is the choice of percussion instruments and their role in the Symphony, rather than the numbers, that has excited comment.
If the Third Symphony charts an 'inner' world, the Fourth, though not impersonal, is more 'public'. This is evident in two related aspects of the work: the external influences, and the diversity of its material.

The year of my Fourth Symphony, 1960, was also the year of the Notting Hill race riots and I was appalled that such a thing could happen in this country. The fact that racial ideas have become increasingly strong in this country dismays me even more. In my Fourth Symphony I have used very obvious West Indian and African percussion instruments and rhythms, in the hope, first, that it sounds well, and second, that it might help to spread the idea of racial integration. This of course is only a small part of the work and is useful for me to know as a composer.[22]

[22] Arnold's programme note

The ethnic aspect of the music is linked with Arnold's love for Bernstein/Sondheim's *West Side Story*, which Arnold saw twelve times after it opened in London in 1958. The last sentence of Arnold's note is very significant. A heartfelt statement of solidarity with ethnic minorities – in itself a brave statement to make at that time – was the springboard for the work and an important aspect of it, but it is a 'small part' of the Symphony as a whole. The work embraces pastoral lyricism, popular song, a longer and even more garish military march than that of the First Symphony and much more. If Arnold's intention had been to cock-a-snook at the critics, he could not have done so more effectively. It provoked a storm of controversy and marked the beginning of Arnold's critical fall from grace.

The Fourth Symphony, perhaps more than any of its predecessors, raises the question of whether the composer is writing 'pure abstract symphonic music' or something programmatic. My instinct is to suggest that there is no hidden programme in the work, and though the listener is free to invent one that fits the music, it would not have been in the composer's mind. Though in some respects the Fourth Symphony anticipates the post-modern poly-stylistic symphonies of composers such as Schnittke and Arho. The cultural references do not amount to pastiche composition; they are absorbed into Arnold's language and, up to a point, into the musical current of the Symphony.

The opening movement is marked *Allegro.* As in the previous two Symphonies there are clear first and second themes, both lyrical, and between them, a theme of transitional character:

Ex. 4a

Ex. 4b

Ex. 4c

The difference here is that each main theme is so distinctive as to appear self-contained; an episode or 'event' that is connected to the current of the movement mainly by a shared tempo and a background of rhythmic ostinati which change character according to the theme that they support. There is a kinship between the rising gestures that launch Ex. 4a and Ex. 4b, and also between the presentation of Ex. 4a and Ex. 4c, both of which are stated first and then re-stated with an imitative counter-melody (almost a strict canon in the case of Ex. 4c). The first subject is one of Arnold's most graceful melodies. Some commentators have remarked upon its 'Englishness'. The transition theme is menacing. Its rhythmic accompaniment, scored for marimba, bongoes,[23] and deep Tom-toms, raises the tension. The second subject explores 1950's dance-hall styles (Victor Sylvester and Edmundo Ros are mentioned by commentators). Arnold upsets the thirty-two bar model for such tunes by writing one that could be heard in two two-bar phrases, but places it so that the opening could be either the up-beat or down-beat. He also teases the listener by seeming to skip a bar midway. The second – canonic – statement merely emphasises the ambiguity.

There are three other thematic elements in the movement, all of them fragmentary:

---

[23] I have followed the spelling 'Bongoes' as they appear in the score of the Fourth, and 'Bongos' in the Fifth Symphony.

Ex. 4d - a scalic figure, which launches the movement:

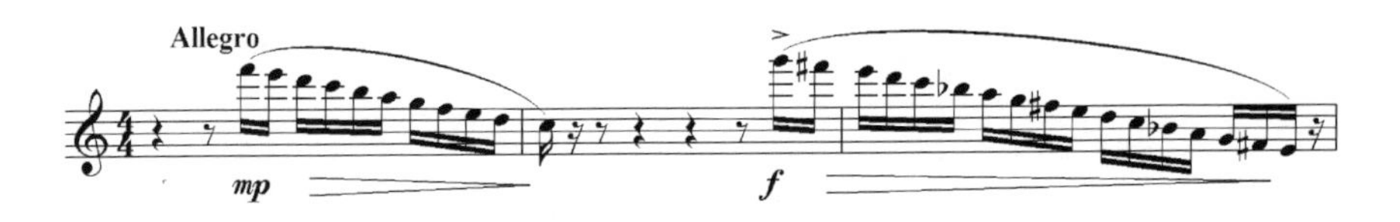

Ex 4e - a rhythmic motif which introduces the Caribbean instruments and their rhythmic style:

Ex 4f - a rhythmic/harmonic motif which is also used in augmentation and diminution:

How does Arnold bind these elements into a coherent form? Not all commentators agree that he does, yet the movement holds one's attention and has a sense of rising tension which, disconcertingly, seems suspended during the long thematic episodes. Arnold's exposition is clearly laid-out and eventful. The introduction – the first in an Arnold symphony that is not linked to the main themes – plays on the ambiguity of the Lydian scale, resting on E, which acts as a leading note to the first subject. At the end of the development a pedal point on F stays in place as the tonic, whilst the surrounding dissonant chord structure dissolves. The development itself is concerned mainly with the fragments (Exs. 4 d-f) but Arnold makes room for a transformed appearance (by augmentation and change of texture) of the first subject, now scored for three trumpets in three-part interweaving counterpoint. Tension is heightened by an increase in tempo and the predominance of Ex. 4b, extended and all but quoting 'Mambo' from *West*

Side Story. In the recapitulation, Arnold re-orders and re-scores the material and further increases the role of the 'fragments'. The first subject has the final word and the movement ends quietly.

The second movement, *Vivace ma non troppo,* is a cunningly proportioned scherzo. The dream-like quality of the 6/8 'A' section, together with the rustic Trio, acts as an escape from the drama of the first movement. The Caribbean instruments are used, but merge with the gossamer web of the orchestral texture, which keeps within a dynamic range ***pp*** – ***mf*** except for the final full-orchestral 'crash' chord on the tonic – A minor. For the first time in a symphony, Arnold adopts the technique of polytonality, made effective by the use throughout the movement of simple modal material, often based on just a few pitches. One passage of particular interest is a three-part canon in keys a major third apart, using one of the many short modal motifs that make up the web of ideas:

Ex 4g

The choice of keys is significant because it anticipates the key scheme of the Trio. The rustic tune of the Trio is heard eight times, in keys a major third apart:

First section	Second Section (palindrome)
Clarinet – A minor	Clarinet – A minor
Oboe – C# minor	Oboe – C# minor
Bassoon – F minor	Bassoon – F minor
Trumpet – A minor	Violins *pizzicato* – A minor

The palindromic treatment of the theme mirrors a loose but effective palindromic ordering of events between the outer sections of the movement. One other point to note is the little rushing scale (upwards near the start, downwards near the end) which echoes Ex. 4d.

The ease with which Arnold writes memorable themes that work naturally in two and three-part canonic imitation is again evident in the *Andantino* third movement. The first is a long melody whose two main phrases (the first introduced by the oboe) are separated by a glowing cadence. These are the phrase openings:

Ex. 4h

The section as a whole has expressive qualities that range from intimacy to tongue-in-cheek sentimentality. Arnold seems to delight in mimicking the post-Wagnerian harmonic clichés of early Hollywood film scores, adding the style to the many 'vernacular' references in the score. The second theme is a slow waltz:

Ex. 4j

The accompaniment becomes ever more exotic in subsequent appearances and at times, through the use of trombone and later, string harmonic glissandi, almost hypnotic. The canonic passages, based on phrases from both themes (sometimes combined) make up the central development section, which reaches a brief climax.

The finale is marked *Con fuoco*. The structural plan of the movement: fugato – march – apotheosis – so closely resembles that of the First Symphony's finale that it could be viewed as a re-run, albeit longer and more colourful.

The first theme is a fugue subject. Each phrase is interrupted by a silence, followed by a three note chromatic figure (a link to the second subject and coda):

Ex 4k

The entries follow the traditional sequence subject-answer-subject – answer and there is a regular counter-subject. The added voices make play with Ex. 4d. As in the fugal finale of the First Symphony, there are more modestly scored counter-expositions, including one for piccolo and two flutes and, most remarkably, a purely rhythmic paraphrase of the process scored for the Caribbean instruments. These passages alternate with the second subject – a lyrical chromatic theme – and a third motif (at **J**) linked to the first movement. The *Alla Marcia* passage has a brashness that verges on brutality. Whereas Arnold transformed his fugue subject to create the First Symphony's march episode, the only connection here is that it picks up and completes the peculiar interruptions to Ex. 4k (X) :

Ex. 4l

The connection is far more tenuous and therefore less effective than the transformation that occurs in the First Symphony. Moreover, the Sousa-like complexion of the march gives the impression that we have stepped out of Arnold's world altogether; a moment of musical graffiti. Some sense of order is restored in the closing *Maestoso* when Arnold sets the fugue subject in slow motion against a timpani ostinato virtually identical to that of the First Symphony's coda. The final bars are marked *Allegro molto* – the opening of the fugue subject hammered out in affirmative repetition in a blaze of Lydian F major.

Arnold's Fourth Symphony has moments of high drama and conflict, as well as a *volte-face* ending. Yet the work can leave the listener with a sense of elation, not least because of Arnold's masterly pacing, control of tonal structure, and use of a network of small related motifs. Arnold's dazzling display of invention in this work is at the highest level thus far in the cycle. But he had yet to reach his full stature.

An English Composer's reply to self-criticism: Symphony No 5 Op. 74 (1961)

Malcolm Arnold's Fourth and Fifth Symphonies were written in close proximity. Recent research[24] gives very persuasive evidence that the date – 1960 – on the MS, which also appears on the title page of the new Novello score[25], is incorrect, and that it was written a year later. The work was commissioned by the Cheltenham Festival Music Society for their 1961 Festival of British Contemporary Music. It was first performed on 3 July 1961 by the Halle Orchestra, conducted by the composer. The Fifth opens a new chapter in the cycle. The following comment from the composer suggests a process of self-evaluation:

After the first performance of my Fourth Symphony there were so many things that I felt needed to be said musically that I am more than grateful for the opportunity given to me by the Cheltenham Festival Society to attempt to say these things.

The music confirms this. The work reveals greater freedom in the handling of symphonic form. In particular:

- Use of explicit thematic cross-reference between movements, giving rise to a stronger sense of integration, making the work a musical journey;
- Less dependence on conventional structural 'signposts' to create a more fluid sense of form (movements 1, 2 and 4);
- Leaner textures and more sparing use of full-orchestral writing;
- Engagement with recherché compositional techniques such as quasi-serial handling of pitch content and the use of ciphers. The use of palindromes, a technique first explored in the Trio of the Fourth Symphony's Scherzo, is extensive.

The Symphony is in the key of E minor. It is essentially a tragic work, in which the composer mourns the recent loss of close friends, all of whom died young:

---

[24] Paul R. W. Jackson: The Life and Music of Sir Malcolm Arnold.

[25] Though the editor acknowledges the new research in an addendum to the latest edition.

- Denis Brain (1921 - 1957) – the great horn player for whom Arnold composed his Horn Concerto No. 2, Op. 58 (1956).
- Gerard Hoffnung (1925 - 1959) – musician, cartoonist and humourist, with whom Arnold collaborated in 1956 and 1958 on the Hoffnung Music Festivals. Arnold's A Grand Grand Overture Op. 57 (1956) was written for the first of these.
- David Paltenghi (1919 - 1961) – former dancer, film director, choreographer and drinking companion.
- Frederick ('Jack') Thurston (1901 - 1957) – clarinettist for whom Arnold composed the Concerto No. 1 for Clarinet and Strings, Op. 20 in 1948.

The work is scored for the 'standard' Arnold orchestra. The large percussion section includes two of the Caribbean instruments first used in the Fourth Symphony (Bongoes, Deep Tom-tom). There are four movements. For the first time in the cycle, Arnold places his Scherzo between the slow movement and the finale.

The Fifth Symphony is not only a deeply felt work, it is a musical journey, held together within a fully functional tonal scheme but combining tonal and non-tonal material within its span to create unrelenting tension and drama. It ranks as one of the most tightly organised symphonies of the Twentieth century. There are no superfluous episodes or textural embellishments. Except for tonal passages in which harmonic/textural support is required, *every note* of the Symphony is related to the basic material of the piece, which consists of:

1. A five-note motif derived from the keys of Arnold's five (up to that point) Symphonies[26]:

Ex. 5a – 'Cycle' motif:

[26] See Anthony Meredith/Paul Harris

Some derivatives of Ex. 5a:

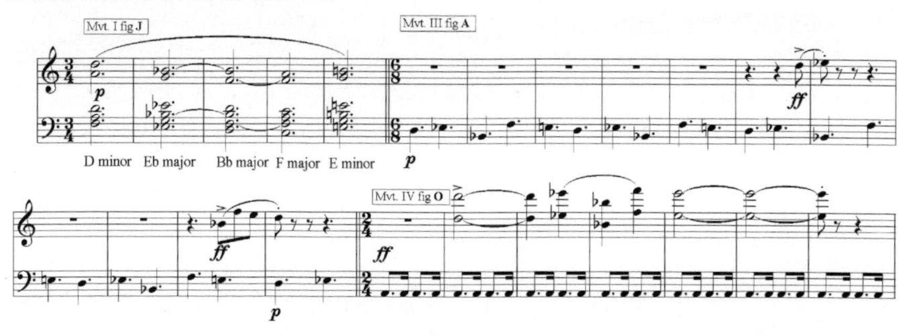

In Ex. 5a, I have highlighted the last note because Arnold gives it greater emphasis in the opening theme of the work, and highlights it throughout the Symphony as a point of arrival. Aside from its symbolic importance as the keynote of *this* Symphony, it becomes a motif in its own right. For instance, at the start of the Scherzo, Arnold omits it from the eight-note pitch complex (see Ex. 50 form A – segment X) and hammers it home at the end of the sequence to announce the key. In the finale he omits it from the reordered tone row, saving it to orientate the music towards the home key. The timpani in particular, tuned to high and low Es, highlight the note, especially in the finale. Here are two examples, the first from bar 38 of the opening movement where it marks the end of the first thematic group and defines the key ahead of a tonal episode; the second from the end of the symphony:

Ex. 5b – Keynote as motif:

The cycle motif is the kernel of the Symphony. Besides its use as a motif, it spells out the three most important keys of the Symphony: E (highlighted) as the key of the whole work, D as the second most important key centre (i.e. the key of the slow movement and the key in which the Symphony seems destined to end until it is wrenched back to E minor in the closing bars), and Bb – the furthest point from E and the main key of the finale's 'march' layer, which runs through almost the entire movement.

Lest anyone thinks that the choice of notes that make up the cycle motif is purely coincidental, further evidence of the connection can be found in the extract below Ex. 5a, taken from **J** in the first movement. Not only is the motif embedded in the chord sequence, but the sequence is built from the key chord of each symphony in sequence, following the major/minor tonality of each:

D minor – Eb major – Bb major – F major – E minor

This sequence of chords plays a vital role in the first movement. Arnold increases the durations of the chords as the movement unfolds and uses it to clinch the final cadence.

2. Two ciphers: GH and AH, sometimes combined as a three note chord. They are the initials of Gerard Hoffnung and his wife Annetta Hoffnung. The pitch material is therefore G/B and AB (H – is the German nomenclature for B). AH is highlighted in the main theme of the slow movement. Ex. 5c shows how Arnold opens out the chord to create a field of Phrygian diatonic harmony, a plateau that acts as an anchor point within the complex tonal scheme of the first movement:

Ex. 5c

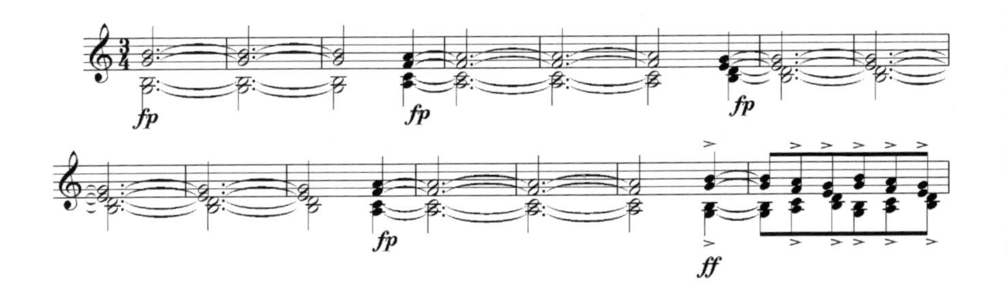

3. A tone row, divided into two segments:

Ex. 5d

The row is consistently divided into two separate segments, marked X and Y. The significance of this is that X excludes the three pitches of the Hoffnung motif, therefore Y completes the row with those notes, plus one other. X is the source of the 'dyad' motif:

Ex. 5e dyad motif

Form A is stated by the trumpet at the start of the finale. I've designated form A as the prime because it is the basis of the dyad motif, which is heard before the arrival of the first movement's cello theme (Ex. 5j), which is based on form B[27] (of Ex. 5j).

Taking segment Y of the row, followed by the bass-line of the dyad motif, Arnold creates a further eight-note segment (B – A# – A – G – C – C# – D – Eb) as the basis of another theme, which is developed across the first,

[27] Which Hugo Cole cites as the row.

third and fourth movements (Ex. 5h). The series is not inverted and is rarely transposed. This is significant because the serial content is heard within the tonal framework of the Symphony as a whole, and therefore functions in relation to the tonal structure. A transposition of the row occurs in the Finale by way of voice-leading towards a brief episode, and is anchored in the dominant (F major) to the key of the main tonal layer (March – Bb major).

4. Four self-contained tonal themes. They are:

- The two main themes of the second (slow movement), of which the first reappears at the end of the Symphony and incorporates one of the ciphers (AH – see below);
- The Trio section of the Scherzo; a comic/grotesque transformation of the non-tonal material that precedes it;
- The Bb major march theme of the finale, which is self-borrowing (from the *Duke of Cambridge March* written for the Royal Military School of Music).[28]

Before I move on to discuss the musical form and narrative of the work, I invite the reader to pause and consider the pleasure that Malcolm Arnold might have taken as he mounted the rostrum to conduct the première of his structural *tour de force* knowing that the critics would fail to recognise it as such. Though it is fair to say that no-one can be expected to hear tone rows, ciphers, retrogrades and transformations as they occur, the sense that something of structural significance is happening is immediately obvious, not least from the clearly recognisable motific cross-references that pervade the symphony and the perception that the music is unlike anything that Arnold had written before. In the event, Arnold received some of the most hostile and unperceptive reviews of his entire symphonic career.

Although the Symphony as a whole expresses a sense of tragedy, the most explicit references to the loss of Arnold's four departed friends are in the first movement. The movement follows a sonata structure but, as in the earlier symphonies, the development and recapitulation are far from predictable. Overall the form is more fluid and elusive than before. The

[28] Noted in Piers Burton Page's biography.

portraits follow the exposition section, rolling development (by way of extension and transformation) and recapitulation into one continuous span.

The movement is marked *Tempestuoso*. It begins with the 'cycle' motif as a plaintive theme for solo oboe:

Ex. 5f

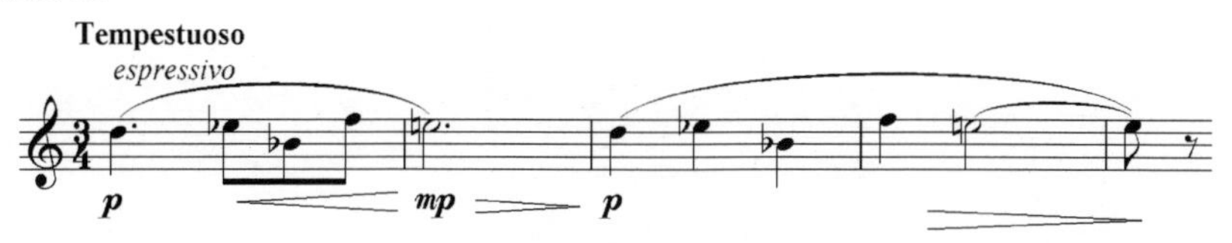

The 'dyads' motif follows immediately, a sense of urgency engendered by its cross rhythms, high dynamic level and brittle scoring (pizzicato strings followed by tuned percussion):

Ex. 5g

From letter **A,** the dyad motif is developed alongside this motif (Segment Y plus the dyad bass-line, developed and later given in rhythmic augmentation):

Ex. 5h

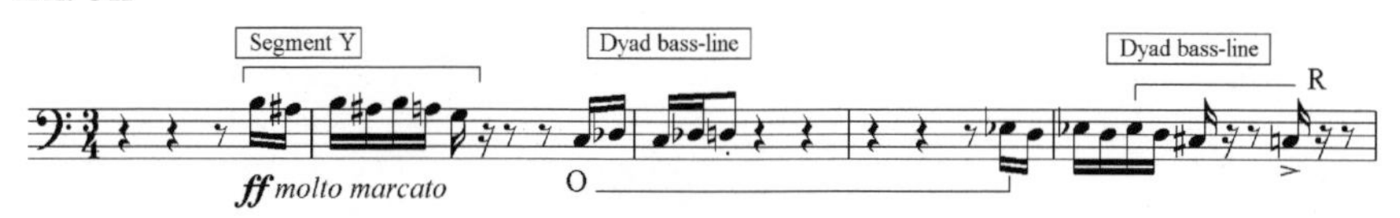

The 'keynote' motif (Ex. 5b) brings the drama of the opening to an abrupt halt. The next section is modal. The 'Hoffnung' motif completes the first appearance of the tonic triad (i.e. E plus G/H = E minor) and heralds a passage of ethereal beauty. The canonic writing for harp and celesta recalls a similarly scored canonic passage from the first movement of the Fourth Symphony:

Ex 5i

The modal harmony is sustained for forty-two bars. The held thirds descend GH – FA – EG, confirming the Phrygian tonality and key chord. This sequence, speeded up into three quavers, becomes an independent motif. A further development is the extension of the sequence through an exquisite chord progression (derived from the 'Cycle' motif) that passes through D minor before returning to E (letter **J**). Ex. 5g intrudes into this episode. Variants of Ex. 5e forge a link to this theme, based on form B of the row, using segment X forward and in retrograde, and the 'cycle' motif at the close. The accompanying chords are derived from the dyads but end with an E minor chord at the arrival of the 'cycle' motif:

Ex 5j

The connection to the opening of the movement (Ex. 5f) is underlined through choice of timbre as the solo oboe takes over the theme (Ex. 5j). Echoes of the 'Hoffnung' episode precede the final statement of Ex. 5j which closes the exposition, via a sudden shift to C major.

The remainder of the movement is Arnold's portrait gallery. In their monographs, Paul R.W Jackson and Anthony Meredith/Paul Harris have identified the biographical links. Dancer/choreographer David Paltenghi is most likely depicted in the wild 'drunken' episode marked *poco piu mosso,* which highlights bass trombone and tuba to comic effect. The episode is based on the 'dyad' motif, as is a later episode (starting at bar 302) whose queasy lurches and violent eruptions might conceivably represent a hangover[29]! The Thurston episode at letter **O** is jazz-inflected; a running bass pattern as the backdrop for a quasi improvisatory solo that retraces Ex. 5j. Dennis Brain is represented by an expansive horn solo, divided into two paragraphs. The material is developed from the 'Hoffnung' episode (Ex. 5i). The great humourist is represented by his own instrument – the tuba – which delivers an augmented version of Ex. 5h. The movement is rounded off by Ex. 5j played by the horn. Phrases that introduced it return once more to create a bitterly intense *fortissimo* climax which ebbs away via the falling thirds to a low G. The timpanist – Ring-master with the 'Key' motif at strategic points throughout these episodes - resolves the harmony to a bass E. Violins unfold the GH motif above it as the music fades into silence (an ending that is revisited at the end of the work).

"*At times of great emotion we speak in emotional clichés*" was Arnold's clarification of an ironic confession made in the first programme note – that he had "*failed to distinguish between sentiment and sentimentality*". The passage that particularly provoked the critics was the theme that opens the second movement:

Ex. 5k (opening)

How sentimental is it? The critics likened it to Hollywood themes, yet the obvious parallel is with the *Adagietto* from Mahler's Fifth Symphony. This is partly a matter of the string scoring, the stillness and simplicity of the accompaniment, and also of the chromatic appoggiaturas that run through

---

[29] One is reminded here of Arnold's score for the film *Hobson's Choice.*

it. The voice, however, is Arnold's. Perhaps that was the problem. The key relationship with the first movement – D major in an E minor Symphony – is another fingerprint; a key a tone below the tonic. In the Ninth Symphony the relationship is reversed. The work is in D major; much of the final *Adagio* sets up an illusion of E minor, making the resolution to D major unexpected. At the end of the finale Arnold repeats Ex. 5h in D major but sidesteps to E minor as its resolution.

A second theme, equally expressive but very different, follows:

Ex. 5l (opening)

The modal simplicity of this melody contrasts with Ex. 5j, as does the orchestration. The bass-line is a three semibreve ground A – E – D which works against the four-bar phrase structure and produces harmonic surprises. We hear the theme three times in succession, each time, the harp/celesta figuration becoming richer and more prominent. A reprise of Ex. 5j, scored this time for woodwind, resolves to the relative minor, ushering in the middle section of the movement. It is launched by a third theme, built from short phrases which Arnold exploits not by repetition but by developing the opening figure (X) towards a sustained climax of tragic intensity. Throughout this section we are reminded, because of their harrowing intensity and melodic shape, of passages from the first two movements of the Third Symphony through Arnold's use of supporting minor chords (5/3 initially, then sevenths) that shift on the down-beat of each bar to form an eight-bar ground:

Ex. 5m

The theme is loosely drawn from segments of form B of the row, allowing some expressive repetition of pitches. It is developed towards a searing climax on this figure derived from the fourth bar:

Ex. 5n

Ex. 5n reappears to clinch the climax of the non-tonal layer beneath the march section of the finale.

The movement is rounded off by its two main themes in reverse order. The textural accretion of Ex. 5i is also reversed. The final quiet orchestral chord is almost identical in scoring to the closing chord of the Ninth. But whereas in the Ninth it is sounds almost unbearably hollow, here it offers a moment of consolation, seemingly without irony.

The marking *con fuoco* underlines the ferocity of much of the Scherzo. The movement flows continuously but the Trio episode stands out because of its tonality and startling change of mood. The Scherzo opens with segment X of form A of the tone row, minus the note E, which arrives 'late' as an E major chord (the first tonic major chord in the Symphony:

Ex. 5o

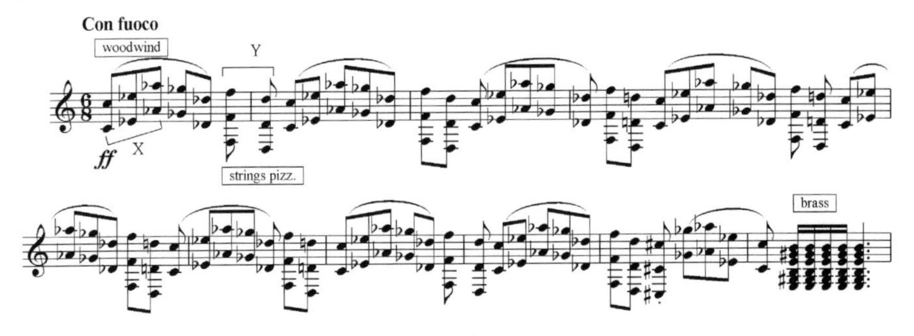

The point of its seven-beat pattern, which confuses the pulse, and its orchestral colouring that hammers home F–D, becomes clear when it is reshaped to form the Trio theme, a pastiche jazz/pop tune over an 'oompah-bass accompaniment',[30] firmly in Bb major with a four-square chord scheme with which it doesn't quite elide rhythmically, using F-D as its melodic punch-line. It is a brilliant musical joke:

Ex. 5p

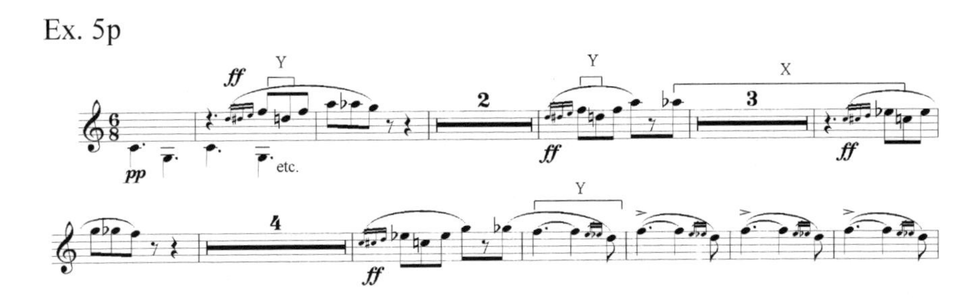

The relationship between the main Scherzo and the exposition of the first movement is easy to follow. After Ex. 5o, we hear the 'cycle' motif (pizzicato cellos and basses), a variant of Ex. 5n and then a *fortissimo* passage based on Ex. 5g transformed into a four-part quasi-fugal passage (subject – subject – answer – subject). The passage has considerable power. Arnold re-runs the Scherzo thus far, but with the events in reverse order, leading to the Trio. The reprise of the Scherzo is much shorter, differently scored and far more dramatic than before (a strategy used in the Scherzo of Symphony No. 4). Only the first bar of Ex. 5o is heard at the end of the

[30] Donald Mitchell: *Malcolm Arnold; The Curse of Popularity*

movement; F-D forcefully contradicted by a fortissimo E scored for full orchestra.

The high drama of the ending continues into the finale, marked *Risoluto*. A quiet trumpet call, based on segment X of form A of the tone row (see Ex. 5d) is answered by Bb/B (from segment Y but harmonised as Bb major/E minor chords) played *fortissimo:*

Ex. 5q

The tritonal conflict between the home key and the key of the March is central to the movement. The main theme, a march, is in Bb major, the furthest tonality from the home key. It is scored for full 'military' effect – for two piccolos (amplified by celesta) and drums (a combination used to magical effect in the first of the English Dances Set II, Op. 33):

Ex. 5r (opening)

The march runs more or less continuously through the main part of the movement (i.e. up to the coda) and creates a tonal layer. Set against it, sometimes at soft dynamic levels, is the non-tonal layer, based on themes and fragments related to the row, and this new motif:

Ex. 5s

This new pitch formation is achieved by taking the four pitches of the march tune, the keynote E and reordering the remaining notes to preserve the basic shape of the dyads:

Ex. 5t

Ex. 5s is the thematic kernel of the movement. It is gradually transformed into a hurtling semiquaver figure, matching the impetus of the march tune, which in turn speeds up and eventually dissolves into blurred figuration. This interaction, the prominence of percussion writing, and the constant interjection of the fanfare figure (Ex. 5d), which is eroded from theme to chords to a mere rhythm on a single note, create the inescapable impression that we are hearing 'battle music'.[31] By saving the 'cycle' motif until the very end of this episode, Arnold achieves the emotional high-point of the drama by recalling the opening of the Symphony. The harmony suddenly shifts to a dominant thirteenth chord of D major, and in blatantly cinematic scoring – a huge crescendo heralds the return of the opening theme of the *Lento*, now *fortissimo.* The scoring could so easily have been overblown if this was meant to be a satirical gesture. It isn't, so we must take it seriously. But D major is not the key of the Symphony. What happens next is aptly described by Donald Mitchell as "one of the most original strokes of the work…a surprising and ruthless twist of the knife."[32] The cadence shifts via

[31] As an experiment, I played a recording of the movement to a mixed group of musicians, and music lovers (some of whom were unfamiliar with Classical music), and asked them to write a single word that could encapsulate what they heard. They all wrote "battle"!

[32] Donald Mitchell: *Malcolm Arnold; The Curse of Popularity*

D# (not D) to resolve on a final E minor chord. The *fortissimo* ebbs away. Tubular bells sound the Hoffnung cipher, and the timpani, once more, complete the chord.

A more detailed analysis of the movement, showing pitch content, motific structure and the pacing of dynamic changes, is given in the Appendix.

Malcolm Arnold's Fifth Symphony has strong claims to be the composer's finest Symphony and perhaps also his finest work. It was the composer's favourite from the cycle. The audience at the first performance did not react as the critics did. The work received a five-minute standing ovation. It was recorded by the composer in 1972 and is, together with Symphony no 2, the most recorded of the Nine. Whether it will ever achieve the place in the international repertoire that it deserves remains to be seen.

Free as a Bird: Symphony No 6 Op. 95 (1967)

Before discussing the problematic Sixth Symphony, I'd like to draw a comparison between the symphonic careers of two composers whose musical aesthetics seem as far apart as it possible to be – Malcolm Arnold and Anton Bruckner. Both composers worked within the 'classical' tradition of the untitled instrumental symphony. Both composed more than nine symphonies but designated nine by numbering the symphonies to form a Beethovenian canon. Both suffered episodes of mental illness and struggled to write their final symphony at a time when their health was impaired. The Fifth Symphony of both composers is a work in which the emotional and structural achievement represents the summation – and more – of the symphonies that preceded them. After writing the Fifth, both composers turned aside from symphonic composition for a brief period. Both Sixth Symphonies were written during a comparatively untroubled period in the composer's life. The resulting work is the Cinderella of the cycle but has its admirers. The Sixth is shorter and seemingly less ambitious than its mighty neighbours and is less often performed (hardly at all in the case of Arnold's). Both are in A major. At this point I must declare my hand and say that I have no doubts about the stature of Bruckner's Sixth, but sense that Arnold's Sixth is uneven, at least in parts, and its artistic intent is elusive, (perhaps intentionally) – hence my designation 'problematic'.

Arnold's first five Symphonies were written within a twelve- year period. The Sixth followed after a gap of five years. It dates from the composer's 'Cornish' period and was completed in July 1967. The first performance took place in Sheffield in 1968 by the BBC Northern Symphony Orchestra under the composer's baton. It was not the big event that the composer hoped for and the critics were dismissive.

The sound-world of the Sixth is unique. The orchestral line-up, like that of the Third Symphony, excludes celesta and harp. Percussion (apart from timpani) is used sparingly and not at all in the first movement.[33] The Symphony lasts around twenty-five minutes, making it the shortest in the cycle. There are three movements. The scheme, like that of Rachmaninov's Third Symphony, incorporates a scherzo episode in the middle (slow) movement. Unusually, Arnold used working titles for each movement. They appear to have been cues to the composer's imagination rather than explicit programmatic ideas. The first movement was headed "The Bird. Free improvisation." The reference is to the great jazz saxophonist Charlie Parker (1920-1955, known as *The Bird*). The remaining movements take their working titles[34] from Berlioz's final symphony *Grande Symphonie funebré et triomphale* ('Funeral March' – 'March Trionfale'). The scheme is, at first sight, an odd mix, to which one must add the pop-music allusions of the scherzo section in the middle of the funereal second movement. And yet we are on familiar ground in Arnold's oeuvre; particularly if we think back to the Second Symphony's funeral march episode and the 'ethnic' elements in the Fourth.

In his book *Malcolm Arnold – A composer of Real Music* – Raphael D. Thöne devotes a chapter to the work, giving a detailed structural analysis and exploring in depth the influence of the music of Charlie Parker. Thöne's work is essential reading for anyone interested in this Symphony. However, though Thöne's sectional breakdown of the first movement is unarguable, I have reached a different conclusion as to the nature of Arnold's thematic organisation (see below).

---

[33] In his programme note Arnold states 'to avoid any suggestion of jazz gimmickry (which I detest) I have not used any percussion other than timpani throughout the movement.'

[34] These titles appear on a page of sketches, which also shows, after 'Funeral March', 'POP, 4477' crossed out.

The first movement is marked *Energico* and is in 4/4 time. The music is unlike anything else in the cycle; dark, edgy, cryptic. If the opening movements of Symphonies 2, 3 and 4 have fleeting 'pastoral' connotations, this music is distinctly 'urban'. Much of this is captured in the rhythmic language of the music, particularly in the widespread use of off-beat accents. Thöne's analysis of the form reveals a notional sonata structure in the context of an episodic sequence of events built on distinctive material. But it is important to note that there is a 'chain' form to the musical discourse of the exposition, and that the stasis of the harmony sometimes works against the sectional divisions to create a conflicting sense of structural boundaries. It is the 'chain reaction' factor that links the music to the working title "The Bird. Free Improvisation".

The movement is not merely a homage to Charlie Parker. It draws on both the fluidity of jazz improvisation in general, and Parker's playing in particular, as well as the element of free dissonance within a tonal context; an element of jazz that offered new creative possibilities at this point in Arnold's exploration of serial techniques. Arnold himself was an accomplished jazz pianist and loved jazz. The handling of pitch material within a tonal context is of particular interest. The movement opens with cascading woodwind figures against a tonic chord (pizzicato strings). The scale used is Octatonic, but related to the part-serial handling of pitch material that follows[35]:

Ex. 6a

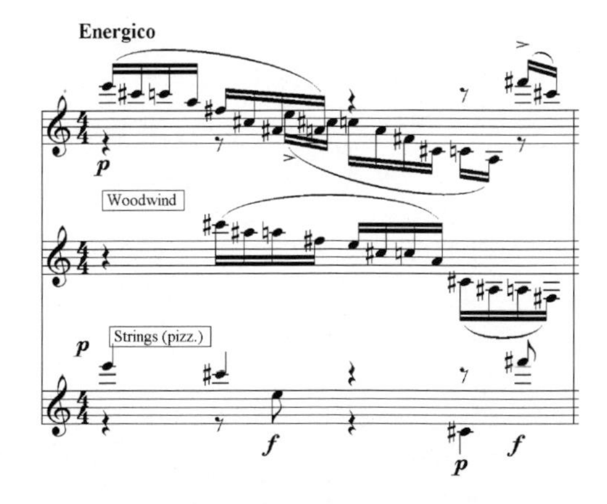

[35] This bar, and its augmented version, fills much of the sketch page.

The first four notes, though seemingly inconsequential, are crucial. Much of the Symphony is concerned with the major/minor third and its tonal implications.[36] Cellos and basses (pizz.) set up a jazzy rhythmic accompaniment with string chords above. The high level of dissonance created here, and which runs through much of the first two movements, is generated by the use of the complete chromatic scale subdivided into two hexachords. The cellos and basses work within a six-pitch formation; the chord above contains all six unused pitches. After fifteen beats the pitch material is switched, completing the sequence:

Ex. 6b

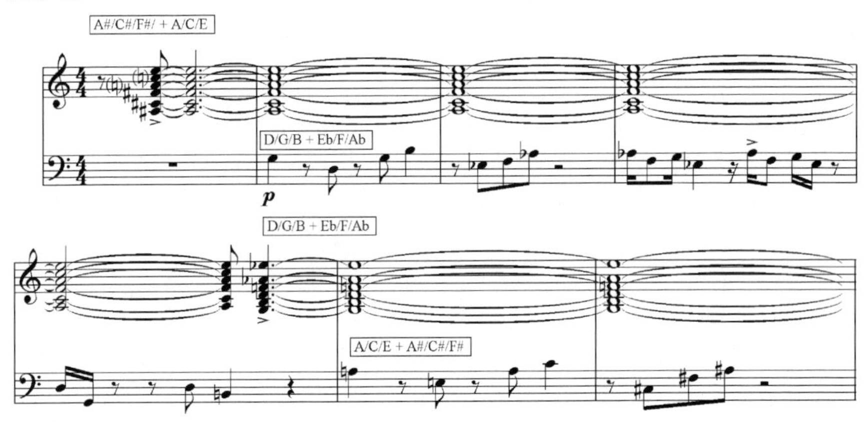

The two chords are in alternation over the course of fifty-four bars of music to create tritonal harmonic tension. The third bar of the cello figure is significant as a rhythmic link to Ex. 6c.

The woodwind tune at letter **A** is aligned to the cello/bass pitch groups but allowed considerable freedom. Of all the material in the movement, this comes closest to Parker's style which stands out by virtue of its melodic independence, and is therefore detached from the 'chain' argument. The thick unison doublings in the woodwind (flutes, oboes and clarinets), normally anathema to the composer, ingeniously emulate the sound of a saxophone. At letter **B,** this embryonic material gels into an arrestingly dark and impassioned theme scored for upper strings;

[36] Christopher Austin has suggested the influence of Mahler's Sixth Symphony here (in conversation with the author).

Ex. 6c (opening)

Throughout this passage, sustained chords launched by violent off-beat *sforzandi* persist. The 'jazz bass-line' becomes a 'walking bass' at letter **C** against which the fragments of the theme develop. The tail-end of Ex. 6c contains the lyrical phrase that opens Ex. 6c, though both use the same alternation of major/minor thirds. The texture finally breaks at letter **D**. It is the change of texture rather than the shape of the theme that creates the sense of a 'second subject'.[37]

Ex. 6d

Two bars of fortissimo bass chords signal the end of the first section of the movement. Here again, Arnold creates clear paragraph endings in such a way that a sonata form is suggested, even though the 'chain' process denies this. As in the previous symphonies, what follows is not straightforward in sonata form terms. From letter **F,** Arnold repeats the section at letter **A** but lightens the scoring. At letter **G** a process of development ensues. An expressive flute solo, drawn from Ex. 6d is followed by an equally expressive oboe solo, accompanied by augmented fragments of Ex. 6a. It bears some resemblance to the material that has gone before. More significant perhaps is its striking similarity to the funereal theme of the slow movement of the Second Symphony:

Ex. 6e opening (see also Ex 2f)

---

[37] Thöne's designation.

Is Ex. 6e a self-quotation and if so, what is its significance? The question highlights the point that Arnold does not rely on 'stock in trade' melodic gestures. The question of self-quotation cannot be answered, though it is interesting to note another, more explicit allusion to the Second Symphony in the middle movement (see below). Violins extend the theme over the same patterns, rising to a *fortissimo* (though lightly textured) climax. The sustained tension of the music is capped by a series of held chords with trills above the 'walking bass', with fragments of Ex. 6c above. The end of the section is marked by the eight fortissimo brass chords, signalling the final phase. The first subject follows immediately. The addition of horns to the string line reminds us once again of the tone of the saxophone, though the effect is achieved by different means. Between Ex. 6c and Ex. 6d comes a large double crescendo; the layered texture builds above repeated dominant (E) timpani crotchets, and is made up of different rhythmic layers and based on the first of the two main chords. It sounds like a long dominant preparation for the recapitulation but its place in the structure denies this. The a-thematic nature of the passage and its extreme length in proportion to the movement as a whole are bewildering in the context of such a thematically developed movement. The effect is like a battering-ram. The 'soloists' appear to have left the stage. A greater sense of climax is achieved in final bars of Ex. 6d, where Arnold once again 'twists the knife'[38] in the climactic phrase extension. A sudden change of dynamic marks the start of the coda, based on the Symphony's first eleven bars. The order of events are reversed. It brings to an end a movement that is unlike anything else in Arnold's symphonic canon. The sustained tension and power of the music is gripping, but perhaps not quite on a par with the first movement of the Fifth Symphony because its outcome is less obviously 'earned' in terms of musical logic.

The second and third movements are also episodic, but conform more closely to classical structures. The ternary *Lento – Allegretto – Lento* movement opens with a high B which returns at strategic points and closes the movement. The movement, therefore, has a pitch centre rather than a home key. However, much of the movement (i.e. the funeral march sections) has a Bb minor tonality. Four haunting chords follow. They accompany one of Arnold's most elegiac themes, which has a 'last post' quality:

---

[38] See Symphony No. 5.

Ex. 6f

As in the first movement, Arnold raises the level of dissonance and tonal ambiguity by drawing the pitches of the theme from those unused in the chord sequence. It is heard three times[39] in the first part of the movement. The scoring changes, leaving a solo trumpet alone in the final statement. The use of canonic imitation for the second statement is another Arnold fingerprint. Instrumental doublings once again emulate the timbres of jazz. Arnold's subtle use of augmentation in phrases of the theme and its chordal accompaniment casts new light on the theme on each appearance. A second strand, just before the final (trumpet) statement of Ex. 6g, is a theme above a funeral march accompaniment:

Ex. 6g

[39] To be strictly accurate, four times if you count the imitative part in the canon, but we hear it as three paced-out statements.

A comparison of this passage and Ex. 2i from the Second Symphony shows a striking similarity. Is it a self-quotation or is the figuration simply 'universal' in character?

The brief 9/8 *Allegretto* stands in complete contrast to the *Lento*. The style is 'popular' (commentators have defined its stylistic origins in different ways). The scoring of the tune is the same as Ex. 6b but in a higher (soprano saxophone?) register. The rhythmic accompaniment is played by pizzicato cellos and basses (as in similar passages in the first movement). The pitch material comprises simple Bb major chords in the accompaniment (organised in attractive seventh chord formations) with the unused pitches reserved for the tune. Snare drum (playing rim shot), tambourine and cymbal (played with side drum stick) recreate the sound of a drum kit:

Ex 6h

At letter **M** the passage comes to an abrupt halt as woodwind and strings hurtle up and down scales in what could be heard as a bizarre parody of Tchaikovskian gestures.[40] The jazz-style resumes for another of the Symphony's ostinato/crescendo passages. Its climax heralds the return of the *Lento.* The funeral march accompaniment runs throughout, supporting both themes, heard in reverse order. Ex. 6f comes only once more, in its canonic form. The movement ends as it began, on a high B, but the effect of a long crescendo cut off by a snare drum rim- shot played ***ff*** is brutal.

The finale is marked *con fuoco*. It is a rondo. The form is as follows:

A	Rondo Theme (played three times)
B	1st episode
A	Rondo Theme (played once)
C	2nd episode

[40] Passages in the finale of the Fourth Symphony and third movement of the Sixth Symphony.

A	Rondo Theme (played once)
D	3rd episode
A	Rondo Theme (played three times)
Coda	A-thematic. Chords IV – V – I

The rondo theme, in triple time (therefore not a march, as suggested in Arnold's working title), has a rugged quality, particularly in the octatonic turns in the melody, and a firmly-anchored tonic pedal. It is unequivocally in the home key - A major. Its heroic intent is underlined by the dactylic rhythm of the string accompaniment with its bold orchestral colouring:

Ex. 6i

We hear it eight times, with changes of scoring across the first five statements.[41] In the first A section, Ex. 6i is played three times – by trumpets (A major), woodwind (Db major) and trombones (F major). The use of keys a major third apart echoes the key scheme of the Trio of the Scherzo of Symphony No. 4. The first episode (B) is very strange. Virtuosic bitonal string figuration breaks off abruptly to be followed by a portentous rhythmic figure, almost Lisztian in character. The third element is a flash-back to the world of the first movement's harmonic tension; ostinati and ***fp*** accents on chords held through a long crescendo. The sequence of small events is repeated. With the return of A (rondo theme) – a single statement – the roles of wind and strings are reversed. The second episode is concerned with fig. X of the rondo theme, which is made darkly comical by the scoring, particularly the jazzy slides of the solo trombone.

[41] The finales of the Fourth and Eighth Symphony follow a similar scheme, but in both cases the re-scorings are more inventive and subtle.

Harmonic tension is high, particularly in a quiet passage that unfolds vertically; a fully chromatic chord of stacked thirds that leaves the piccolo shimmering on repeated high C#s. The sequence of events is loosely palindromic. The third A section is the quietest; timpani solo with percussion, a solo bassoon supplying the notes of the tune that the timpani cannot play. The third episode (D) is a highly effective 'mini-passacaglia' on an eight-bar chord sequence. There are just three 'variations', each building on the melody first played by upper strings and horns. The dynamic level rises gradually. The passacaglia theme sets up the necessary tonal orientation to prepare the return of the home key as the resolution of its harmonic tensions. Its repetitions thus delay resolution to strengthen the effect of the tonic chord when it finally arrives. The final section of the rondo is an exact repetition of the opening section, without changes of scoring. By Arnold's standards this is disappointing. Surely this was the place to create some sense of a journey's end; something that Arnold had the skill to do through orchestration alone, had he wanted to. But did he? The twenty-five bar coda gives us a lengthy IV – V – I cadence; a blaze of sound that recalls the endings of Symphonies 1 – 4 without adding anything fresh. It feels strangely hollow and fails to erase the brooding drama of the first movement or the funereal second. Perhaps that was Arnold's intention. In this respect, the journeys of Arnold's Sixth and Eighth Symphonies are very similar, though the latter strikes a deeper note.

Malcolm Arnold broke new ground in the Sixth Symphony but the work as a whole is uneven. Nevertheless, it is a brave new step in the direction of the last three symphonies, and all four silence any accusation that Arnold was concerned with playing to the gallery.

Family matters: Symphony No 7, Op. 113 (1973)

Tippet's Symphony No. 3 (1972) and Arnold's Symphony No. 7 (1973) occupy a comparable place in each composer's symphonic canon. Both are bigger, bolder, more dynamic, more complex and more impassioned than anything that went before. There are similarities in the sound-world of each piece: repetition of small fragments built into 'mosaics' within a structure that also embraces stretches of powerfully scored lyrical writing; little sense of functional tonality as a means of carrying the musical journey; prominent percussion writing using unusual sounds that have symbolic meaning; and unparalleled demands in terns of orchestral virtuosity. Both works – whether or not one accepts them as representing the level of symphonic coherence achieved before and after – command attention, and make an overwhelming impression in performance. Neither symphony can be approached as an abstract symphonic work. Tippett's programme is explicit. The work concludes with a vocal finale[42] and makes (through reference to Beethoven's Ninth) its statement of the composer's world view. Arnold's vision is more personal. The symphony is dedicated *to Katherine, Robert and Edward* – the composer's three children. The dedication matches the order of the movements, one devoted to each child. Paul R.W Jackson has deduced from the composer's sketches that the use of ciphers is extensive. Arnold encodes the names of his three children, his two wives and his own name, sometimes partnering them. It is important to note that the complex encryption system that Arnold invented allows a choice of outcomes; therefore the musical material is not entirely the result of 'chance' procedures. The use of ciphers runs though the whole Symphony, and names are not exclusive to each child's movement. Then there is the symbolic use of a large cowbell at the end of each movement – ominous to the uninitiated; a symbol of hope according to the composer.[43] Commentators – most notably Jackson and Meredith/Harris – have illuminated the private world (including hidden programmatic elements) of the work as far as seems possible. Their commentaries on the Seventh are therefore essential reading for anyone who wants to explore the work. But where does this leave the listener who approaches the work as an untitled three-movement instrumental symphony with only a dedication to go by? One might argue that, with the possible exception of the Third and Ninth, there is no such thing as an 'abstract' Arnold symphony. The closest relative of the Seventh is the Fifth – a work that includes portraits of friends and uses 'symbolic' pitch material that the listener would not be able to detect. But that is only one part of a work that grips the listener through its unflagging energy and compositional discipline. The balance between the personal and a universal experience is much more problematic in the Seventh. Its essence is the composer's willingness to confront his personal demons. The result is a work of intense – sometimes violent – emotional power, and is deeply involving on that level.

The symphony was commissioned by the New Philharmonia Orchestra and was premiered at the Royal Festival Hall London on 5 May 1974 with the

[42] The text is by the composer.
[43] The composer's programme note.

composer conducting. The reviews were mixed (as opposed to universally hostile or virtually non-existent) with some acknowledgement that Arnold had extended his symphonic horizons and made an impact on the audience. After the Sixth, the gap between symphonies continued to be around five to seven years. Arnold's film career was over and his composing career stopped altogether in 1990. To write the Seventh he sought seclusion, staying, initially, with the Waltons on Ischia until an unfortunate confrontation impelled him to return to Ireland where he was then living. It was a turbulent and busy period for the composer but the Symphony was completed fairly quickly. The Seventh is not the composer's longest Symphony. It lasts around forty minutes[44] as opposed to the Ninth, which lasts over fifty. But the length of the Ninth is down to the slow pace of the final movement, which follows movements on a smaller scale. The canvass of the Seventh has an altogether different feel, and reminds us, in the ambition and drama of its musical argument, and in its voice, of Mahler and Shostakovich. The Sibelian model is therefore far behind, except in terms of the orchestral forces deployed. They are the same as for Symphony No. 2, plus a third percussionist, though it requires the largest array of percussion used in an Arnold symphony.

In his handling of tonality, Arnold moves even further away from conventional notions of key than he did in the Sixth. There is a key centre – F major – but it is barely discernable at the start of the outer movements and is confirmed only at the end of each, but without any real sense of affirmation. In the outer movements there is a strong pull towards A major. The first movement – *Allegro Energico* – is Arnold's longest opening movement. Although this is Katherine's movement, it begins with the ciphers for Arnold's three children, followed by the other ciphers in an introductory section that is violent in character and punctuated by strange comic/grotesque dance-gestures:

[44] There are accounts of performances lasting up to 45', and the length varies considerably between recordings.

Ex. 7a

Ex. 7b

The opening notes F – A – Bb appear later in double augmentation as an independent motif. Ex. 7a has a searing quality. Ex. 7b is radiant and energetic, the three note tail figure notable for its 'airborne' leaps. Note the obligato bass-line, not (it seems) a cipher and used to add 'spare' pitches to enrich the harmony. The material unfolds at some length and the sequence is repeated, with Ex. 7a more lightly scored and Ex. 7b in rhythmic diminution; a tremendous burst of energy. Interruptions occur as Arnold sustains a succession of high and low pitches without establishing a firm sense of key. The last of these – a piercing high A – acts as a leading note to Bb minor. The main theme of the movement follows:

Ex. 7c (opening)

The theme is the longest in an Arnold symphony. Its yearning quality is emphasised in the simple harmonies that shift between major and minor chords, edging towards an A major resolution that, in the context of what has gone before, seems like a vista of hope and is met by a fanfare-like figure derived from the Katherine motif. The theme is repeated, differently scored and disturbed by the dance rhythm. Such is the length of the theme that changes of scoring and texture can occur that break it down into separate episodes, as here, when a solo horn carries it thorough to a brief development, followed by an explosive *fortissimo* passage on Ex. 7b in diminution. The third statement of Ex. 7c begins a process of expansion and development, reaching into the centre of the movement. We hear all of the above material in different lights as the music proceeds towards its midway point. There is a wealth of detail here, much of it seemingly significant in relation to the ciphers. The boundaries of sonata form are unclear, although the appearance of this off-shoot from Ex. 7c has a 'codetta' feel:

Ex. 7d (opening)

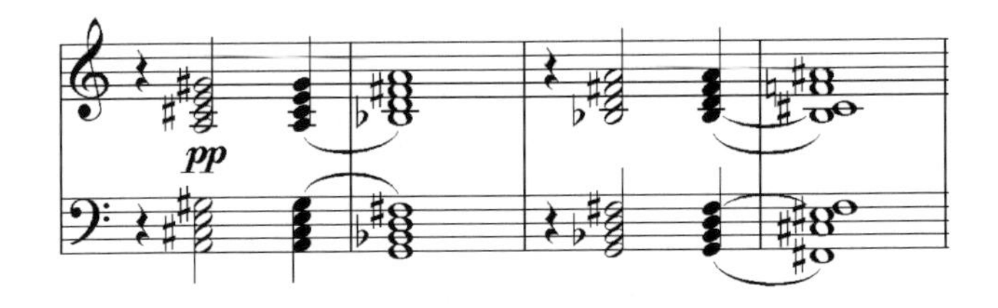

Ex. 7d briefly confirms the A major key centre reached at the end of the main theme and breathes an air of serenity. It proves deceptive. The main theme (Ex. 7c) comes again but is joined by a 'jazz trio' of clarinet, trombone and percussion who offer a bizarre parody of ragtime. The main development ensues; a huge expansion of the cipher material in a strange partnership with long pedal points of repeated semiquavers, which sometimes drive the music and at others, threaten to envelop it. The inexplicable interplay of ciphers and small motifs throughout this section, not to mention the jazz parody that precedes it, is so rich in hidden programmatic references that the listener might be forgiven for wanting to hear a performance given with surtitles! A fully scored reprise of the main theme proves cathartic. It is followed by the expanded third statement, leading to the codetta theme (Ex. 7d). Throughout this passage Arnold provides potent harmonic changes to the original statements. The calm is shattered by a full reprise of the opening paragraph of the Symphony. It settles on an augmented-second chord – Gb/A – with added dissonance, and spread between the extreme heights and depths of the orchestra; the bass note Gb propelled by semiquavers. Despite the careful preparation through voice-leading, the resolution to a low unison F is totally unexpected as an outcome to the movement. The sound of a large cowbell makes its first appearance, and returns towards the end of each movement.

In purely autobiographical terms it is difficult to know what to make of Katherine's portrait, not least because of its moments of harrowing violence and because of the inclusion of all of the names as ciphers. As a symphonic movement it proves Arnold's ability to work successfully on a much larger canvass than before. Though at times it feels episodic, it works, despite the lack of conventional tonal relationships, because of the vividness and potency of its ideas and their dramatic pacing.

Robert's portrait forms the second movement, marked *Andante con moto*. The movement is hauntingly expressive. It opens with swaying chords (Ex.7e) that act as a backdrop for the first of two long soliloquies, played by the trombone[45] (Ex. 7f - opening)

Ex. 7e

[45] Perhaps this movement, rather than the slow movement of the Sixth, is Arnold's real answer to the slow movement of Berlioz's *Grande Symphonie funebré et triomphale.* Berlioz places a solo trombone in the role of orator, as does Arnold.

Ex. 7f

The trombone's falling chromatic lines work against rising chromatic lines in the strings, above a held C major chord. The three together create a beguiling harmonic effect. The second soliloquy is given to unaccompanied violas. The scoring and dynamic are reminiscent of the opening of Mahler's Tenth Symphony, whilst the melodic line bears a curious resemblance to the opening theme of the slow movement of Bruckner's Seventh. The latter is surely coincidental for, as Paul R.W. Jackson has shown, its shape is derived from the ciphers ROBERT – MALCOLM:

Ex 7g

The trombone theme is freely developed by three trumpets. They climb to a high chord, which ushers in an eerie episode. Trumpets and trombones exchange cluster chords whilst bongos, timbales and a conga drum tap out, first, a four note quaver rhythm, and then a ten-note semiquaver rhythm. Harmonic stasis suddenly abates as Ex. 7g is played by the trombone. As Arnold retraces his material, reordered and rescored, the music reaches a searing climax once again (as in the first movement) propelled forward by a driving semiquaver rhythm. The symbolic cowbell tolls the end of the movement's main argument. The full orchestra exclaim Ex. 7e, and the trombone soloist has the last word with Ex. 7f played against an eerie string tremolando accompaniment. The last note is a low F#, which confirms the tonal structure that flows from the bass note of Ex. 7e and anchors the great climax near the end.

Edward, Arnold's youngest son, who suffered from autism, is portrayed in the final movement. The movement is the shortest, gentlest and most intimate of the three. The most touching link between father and son, one that the listener cannot miss because it stands apart from the music of the Symphony at every level (style, thematic unity, and structural logic) is the 'Irish' episode near the end – an evocation of the group *The Chieftains* that the young Edward was fond of.

The movement is a rondo. The main theme is drawn from Edward's name and is rhythmically driven. The tonality is unsettled but the theme is launched from the Symphony's as yet nebulous keynote. The theme eludes any sense of an established key and is concerned with the EDWARD cipher:

Ex. 7h

We hear it three times, differently scored and with a brief episode between the second and third statements of the theme, which maintains the driving dotted rhythms. The B section presents two themes, both lightly scored but of high intensity, and bound together by this accompanimental figure that runs like a seam through the section and links into the second episode:

Ex. 7i

Used in rhythmic diminution, Ex. 7i drives the music to a brief but stormy climax before the second A section. The rondo theme is heard twice more. Arnold follows his familiar strategy of presenting the rondo theme in different colours and lighter scoring. Ex. 7i is picked up by lower strings (violas and basses) and the time signature changes to 6/8. The 'Irish' episode begins with a solo for harp, later joined by piccolo, against eerie brass chords – an echo of the 'cluster chord' episode from the second movement. The harp melody (Ex. 7j) appears to be pure pastiche, as does the whole of the A major second section (*Allegro)* which represents the full sound of an Irish folk-band, complete with the tenor drum in imitation of the *bodhran.*

Ex. 7j (opening)

The second half of the Irish episode reaches a grand *accelerando* but dissolves into a tiny reprise of the harp solo. The opening bars of the movement make a sudden return, and after a very brief climax, a quiet chord shifts towards the final F major resolution. Three loud strokes of the large cowbell are answered by a massive F major full-orchestral chord and a final rhythmic echo of the cowbell rhythm.

The ending of the Seventh seems strangely perfunctory. One reason for this is that the home key of F major plays such a peripheral role in the work, perhaps intentionally, because the focus of the work is so highly personal – therefore strong tonal orientation as the focal point of the musical journey might distract from it. The last movement as a whole is small-scale in comparison with the preceding movements. The movement is lower-voltage than the others, and what voltage it has is almost completely discharged in the 'Irish' episode, which disappoints, not because of its ethnic character but because it is essentially pastiche; far more so than any other 'vernacular' reference in an Arnold symphony. Perhaps these comments arise from expectations based on absolute music. This isn't absolute music, but it isn't presented as programme music either. Can Arnold have it both ways? That has to be for each listener to decide. Whatever the response, the listener can hardly fail to be moved by the Seventh Symphony. It is, as Piers Burton-Page describes it[46], "music of the utmost power and intensity".

---

[46] Piers Burton-Page: *Philharmonic Concerto: The life and Music of Sir Malcolm Arnold.*

Lyric Interlude: Symphony for Brass Op. 123 (1986)

Amongst the unnumbered Symphonies by Malcolm Arnold, the Symphony for Brass has the strongest claim to be seen as a major work, but it has little in common with the numbered symphonies that form the cycle.

The Symphony for Brass was written, as the dedication tells us, *For Philip Jones on his Fiftieth Birthday*. Paul R.W. Jackson has pointed out that Arnold's manuscript is unusually messy, which suggests a difficult 'birth' to the work. This coincides with the circumstances of the work's composition. The work (along with the Eighth Symphony – written immediately afterwards), comes from the most troubled period in the composer's life (see below).

If there is a greater composer/trumpeter than Malcolm Arnold in the history of music, I haven't heard of him/her, therefore a Symphony for Brass by such a figure must be reckoned as an event in its own right. The work is less appealing and accessible than Arnold's popular Quintet for Brass Op. 73, but it is of greater stature. It has not secured a prominent place in the repertoire for ten-piece brass. The technical difficulty of the writing may be a factor, although an aspect of brass playing is that through a combination of improved training and instrument design, each new generation of players seem able cope with technical challenges that once only a few virtuosi could surmount, so it is likely that this barrier will eventually disappear.

The Symphony for Brass is a four-movement work which has its own unique sound-word but bears the hallmarks of Arnold's late style, particularly the passages of exposed and astringent two-part writing, sections that are dissonant and/or tonally ambiguous (including some bitonal writing) and the seeming abandonment of the work's emotional journey in the finale. This aspect is highlighted by the work's most unusual feature. It does not declare the home key (Bb) until the final movement. Though one might therefore talk of 'progressive tonality' in relation to the work, there is nothing in it to compare with the concept of progressive tonality as the driving force of a musical journey, as heard, for instance, in Nielsen's Symphonies.

The Symphony's opening defines the tonal instability of much of the work and has a rare beauty that seems to flow from Arnold's memories of certain types of harmonic progression in jazz. The form of the first movement, defined in basic terms by the sequence of time signature and tempo changes, is A – B – A (*Allegro Moderato* 4/4 – *Vivace* 12/8 – *Allegro Moderato* 4/4). However, the material is developed across the movement. The final cadence is in C major, but one senses that the music simply happens to be in that key at the point when Arnold decided to call an abrupt halt. The *Allegretto grazioso* second movement presents simple minuet-like ideas in an emotionally ambiguous context, with much emphasis on small group writing and some use of canon. The third movement – *Andante con moto* – has a weighty opening statement that might have been suitable for treatment as a passacaglia theme but is used as a ritornello between lightly accompanied soliloquies. The finale – *Allegro con brio* – makes use of rhythmically buoyant material that is more obviously in keeping with traditional styles of writing lively music for brass, but maintains a high level of dissonance and tension at certain points. nevertheless, the movement feels like a retreat from the uncompromising style of the previous movements.

Poised between the agonies of the Seventh and Eighth Symphonies, the Symphony for Brass is a subdued work of elusive beauty and undemonstrative vitality.

On the edge: Symphony No. 8, Op. 124 (1978)

Arnold's Eighth Symphony was commissioned by the Rustam K Kermani Foundation for the Albany Symphony Orchestra, New York. It received its premiere on 5 May 1979 in Albany. The Eighth comes from one of the darkest periods in Arnold's life. Recently returned from Ireland, the composer was a patient at the Royal Free Hospital in London where he received treatment following a suicide attempt. The creative will to write, first the Symphony for Brass Op. 123 and then the Eighth Symphony (both commissioned), by absenting himself on a daily basis to return to his studio and compose, represents an artistic triumph. Symphony No. 8 is a fine work but it has not fared well since its first performance, and awaits a professional UK performance in a major venue.

The work is shorter and seemingly less ambitious than its predecessor, but I don't hear it – as Hugo Cole does – as "a lightweight work".[47] The first

[47] Hugo Cole: *Malcolm Arnold – An Introduction to his Music.*

movement is nightmarish, the second is calmer but with unsettling episodes. The finale is punctuated by passages of bewildering austerity and dissonance that negate the jubilant mood and do nothing to dispel the strange contradictions of the previous movements.

The opening *Allegro* defies simple structural analysis. There is the ghost of a sonata form, mainly thematic and contradicted by the key structure, which articulates but does not resolve the clash between the home key – D major – and the remotest point –Ab. The conflict is embedded in the movement from the opening bar onwards. The music operates on two unconnected layers. If, simply for the sake of analysis, one may separate the two, there is a main layer, which is launched by what passes for a first thematic group made up of fragments: D major fanfares, thunderous timpani chords and wailing semitone figures. A figure that appears at letter **C** assumes growing significance as the movement unfolds:

Ex. 8a

Note the quasi-serial construction here. Without the repeated C this would be a text-book twelve-tone theme. It is expanded in a quiet passage at letter **E**:

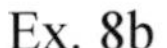
Ex. 8b

The theme passes from flute to lower strings then upper strings, and undergoes some transformation along the way. There are hints of a march rhythm in the accompaniment. The opening chord suggests the arrival of the dominant key but it is too unstable to define a functional key relationship. The fragments are developed at some length and there is a truncated recapitulation starting just before letter **L** The climax (letter **M**) is articulated by a string theme loosely based on Ex. 8b. A further (and longer) transformation played quietly by clarinets (letter **O**) concludes the argument, such as it is.

The other layer, utterly incongruous and unrelated to what goes on around it, is a sixteen-bar Irish march, rescored[48] but otherwise lifted (complete with conventional harmonies and dominant/sub-dominant key changes) from Arnold's score for the film *The Reckoning*. The film is set in London and Liverpool, but it concerns a man's growing sense of allegiance to his Irish roots. The composer, who left Ireland shortly before writing the Eighth, denied any hidden programme to the Symphony connected to Irish politics.[49] Amongst the sketches is a copy of the sheet music for the march[50] annotated with the composer's ideas for rescoring it for use in the Symphony. On the front cover, Arnold has written "1st Movement…Sweet Ireland". Could it be that Arnold is expressing his nostalgia for his temporary homeland?

Ex. 8c (opening)

As if to emphasise the surreal nature of its appearance, Arnold sets up an Ab pedal point near the start of the movement and holds it for eighty-four bars, grinding against the D major tune and, especially, the simple harmony of its accompaniment. We hear the march tune twice; first flute and then harp. The next appearance comes midway through the development section, this time scored for full orchestra against a swaying ostinato figure in Ab. It comes again part-way through the recapitulation (solo bassoon against a dissonant G minor 11th chord played by the harp) and at the end of the movement, assigned to the piccolo, with *almost* consonant harmony[51] (it is

---

[48] The rescoring is gentler than the film theme. There the march is led by the trumpet and sometimes presented in syncopated rhythm to match the style of the jazzy music that surrounds it.
[49] Piers Burton-Page: *Philharmonic Concerto: The life and Music of Sir Malcolm Arnold.*
[50] Screen Gems-Columbia Music Limited.
[51] The main clash occurs in bar 7 of the tune (G/G# in the harmony). It is *just* possible that this is an error in the score.

important that the dissonances are heard in performance because they are Arnold's way of not over-playing his hand whilst keeping the surreal effect alive). The martial accompaniment sometimes outlasts the sixteen-bar phrase and fades into silence as the main layer resumes. Although Ex. 8c seems at first to assume the role of a second subject because of its simplicity and major tonality, that is not its role. It is always in the tonic, and its placement in the movement does not have a clear structural role except possibly to provide an initial – and extreme – contrast to the opening. The movement defies conventional notions of form and content. It is an unfulfilled symphonic drama, constantly put on hold whilst the ghost of a patriot army marches across its landscape.

The central *Andantino* offers some sense of consolation, its tender opening theme reminiscent of the slow movement of the First Symphony (see Ex. 1d):

Ex. 8d

Despite the C major harmony of the opening, the movement is in E Phrygian.[52] As in the First Symphony, Arnold suspends cadential resolution until the very end of the movement. Two small elements of the accompaniment – the little rhythmic motif (X) and the sliding horn figure (Y)[53] – are highlighted in this example because they are developed

[52] The sketch is headed 'Satie (Phrygian mode)'. Why Satie? Perhaps Arnold associated Satie with the colour/character of the Phrygian mode.

[53] Fig. Y is highlighted in the sketch.

independently as the movement unfolds. The theme is one of Arnold's finest inspirations, particularly the harmonic shifts, which foreshadow the darker episodes that follow. We hear it twice, the second time played by solo oboe, with added harmonic subtleties beneath. At figure **B,** a short passage for low brass and timpani creates a funereal mood. Unison strings enter with a new phrase, which includes the rhythmic motif X:

Ex. 8e

Note too the emphasis of the falling and rising semitone as an echo of Ex. 8d. It continues into the main theme, sparsely supported by a single line that contradicts the harmony. Ex. 8f reappears in ghostly colouring. A solo bassoon restates the opening theme, the harmony darkly distorted. Two variants follow: a duet for horn and tuba incongruously set against a G major chord for harp and timpani, and a unison statement for strings, which leads back to the G major chord, this time set up as a 'music box' ostinato[54] with added glockenspiel and vibraphone. Unison horns declaim a variant of fig. Y (Ex. 8d) A sudden fortissimo erupts. The coda extends the short funereal episode and brings the movement to a close, confirming the E Phrygian tonality.

The finale is marked *Vivace*. After two movements that are emotionally, tonally and structurally perplexing, Arnold's masterstroke is to end with one of his most brilliant but deceptively simple dance movements, set in a form that is so schematic as to be devoid of any connecting tissue at all. The juxtaposition of the rhythmically vibrant and harmonically scintillating main theme, with episodes of painfully bleak two and three-part writing based on tonally un-centred themes, leaves the listener in no doubt as to the hollowness of the jubilation. Not even a token fifteen-bar coda of a-thematic tonic/dominant harmony (with echoes of the earlier symphonies in the timpani ostinato and as empty as the coda of the Sixth) can banish the impression.

---

[54] The sketch is headed 'music box – not Boulez or Tippett!' and later 'G major ostinato Lonely Romantic Nostalgia'.

The sixteen-bar main theme follows a simple harmonic pattern[55]:

Ex. 8f

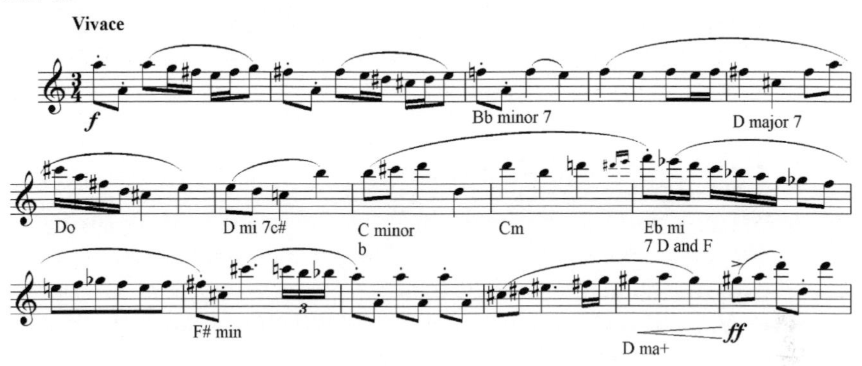

The movement is a rondo:

A	• Rondo Theme: high woodwind with string accompaniment • Rondo Theme: middle-range woodwind, horns and strings with brass/percussion accompaniment • Rondo Theme: flutes/oboes with string accompaniment
B	• Theme B: woodwind chords + string melody • Theme B: string chords + trumpet melody
A	• Rondo Theme: first violins with string accompaniment • Rondo Theme: unison horns and clarinets with string accompaniment
C	• Theme C: (22 bar unaccompanied duet) for 1st/2nd violins • Theme C: (22 bar unaccompanied duet) for violas and cellos
A	• Rondo Theme: solo vibraphone with harp/percussion accompaniment
D	• Theme D (8 bars): clarinet (unaccompanied) • Theme D (8 bars): flute with clarinet • Theme D (8 bars): oboe with flute and clarinet • Theme D (8 bars): bassoon with clarinet • Theme D (8 bars): trumpet (unaccompanied) • Theme D (8 bars) : trumpet duet
A	• Rondo Theme: solo bassoon with timpani • Rondo Theme: full orchestra
Coda	A-thematic passage on tonic/dominant harmony: full orchestra

---

[55] The chord symbols are presented as they appear in Arnold's sketch.

The scoring of the rondo theme changes with every statement, a strategy rehearsed in the Sixth Symphony but carried off here with greater imagination. Note too the scheme of the contrasting sections, which also matches the structure of the Sixth's rondo. The final D section is built from short phrases, the previous sections from more substantial material. The soloistic scoring across the movement as a whole creates a *concerto for orchestra* effect – the unison horn/clarinet and vibraphone panels in the A sections in particular are high-wire acts of daring for the players. Arnold phases his reduction of forces and dynamics across the whole movement, a kind of Malcolm Arnold *Farewell Symphony* finale, the illusion shattered by the sudden *fortissimo* tutti and coda. The shifting syncopated chords of the B section maintain something of the harmonic richness of the rondo theme. The C and D sections are notable both for their textural austerity and dissonance. The C section draws on this quasi-serial approach[56]:

Ex. 8g

Ex 8g shows Arnold's familiar practice[57] of presenting tonal material against unused pitches. The treatment of pitch material in the C section is less systematic than before but one can hear that moments of extreme dissonance are achieved at points where the two segments are laid bare:

[56] The word 'series' and this pitch formulation appear in the sketches with the upper line marked 'phrygian transposed'.
[57] See Symphony No 5 and Symphony No 6.

Ex. 8h

The D section is launched by solo clarinet, joined by flute, then oboe, then bassoon. The sequence is then passed to three trumpets entering one after the other and ends with horn and tuba. The exposed scoring has a chilling effect. The movement as a whole demonstrates Arnold's ability to sustain a structure on statement alone. In this respect it breaks new ground and anticipates the Ninth Symphony.

The Eighth is one of Arnold most undervalued and misunderstood Symphonies. It is a fascinating work, which has a torn, disoriented quality offset by vibrant energy of the finale. The work's inner world of expression is, by turns, tender and harrowingly bleak. So too is the world of Arnold's final Symphony, the Ninth, but the music could hardly be more different.

Surrender to despair: Symphony No 9 Op. 128 (1986)

If there is such a thing as music written 'beyond the grave' we cannot hear it, though anyone listening to Derek Cooke's reconstruction of Mahler's Tenth Symphony might be forgiven for imagining that they can. But there are cases – Arnold's Ninth Symphony and Alfred Schnittke's Ninth – of works written by composers who had suffered a lifetime of debilitating illness, whose final symphonic testament was written against all odds, resulting in works that are pared down to the barest essentials. Schnittke's infirmity was essentially physical. Arnold's infirmity, the result of years of damaging medical treatment, affected his mental capacity on certain levels, especially his ability to write anything beyond two-part (plus, very occasionally, simple three-part) counterpoint, block chords, and repeated statements without extended development.

The circumstances of the work's composition are well documented: a commission that lapsed after a catastrophic breakdown following the composer's most determined suicide attempt; a long period of recuperation; the composer's meeting with Anthony Day (the work's dedicatee) who then became his lifelong carer and created the conditions that enabled the composer, now disabled, to resume composition after a long silence; the consternation that greeted the score; its initial rejection and eventual workshop performance that led to a recording.

Was Arnold, like Bruckner and Mahler before him, haunted by the significance of reaching the magic number nine to complete his cycle? There are parallels between Arnold's symphonic cycle and Beethoven's: a boldly original First Symphony; a more expansive Third; an epic Fifth and Seventh; a shorter, seemingly relaxed Eighth. The composition of a Ninth Symphony, on a larger scale than its predecessors, one that should break new ground and be more searching and profound than anything that had preceded it, would therefore meet the highest expectations. In many ways, Arnold's Ninth fits that description, but it is built on simple ideas presented with the greatest imaginable austerity. The expressive power of the work therefore lies in some of Arnold's most potent musical gifts; the power of simple, instantly memorable themes, their placement within the framework of the Symphony and the way in which different orchestral colourings lend meaning to their many reprises, and effective contrapuntal writing. The manner is therefore more direct though simpler than before, taking up an approach to symphonic thinking that is already evident in the finale of the Eighth Symphony. Had Arnold composed the Ninth immediately after the Eighth (as he was due to do) before his breakdown, the work would surely have turned out differently. Without hearing a note of the Ninth but knowing the circumstances of its creation, one may be moved by the very fact that it exists at all. Hearing it, some listeners will find it to be a heroic failure, the composer firing on less than four cylinders writing a work that is fluent but seems to meander through long stretches of texturally barren writing whilst meeting the basic requirements of the composer's formal models. Others (myself included) hear it as a work in which the composer achieves a new purity and directness of expression that is sufficient to carry a depth of meaning well beyond the seemingly fragile content on the page.

The Ninth is in four movements. The ground plan places it in a line of succession that includes Tchaikovsky's Sixth (Pathetique) and Mahler's Ninth. For the first time in the cycle Arnold ends with a slow movement. It is the heart of the work and lasts roughly as long as the preceding movements put together. The lightness and relative brevity of the opening movements are very different to the drama played out in the first three movements of Tchaikovsky's and Mahler's last completed symphonic works. A work that comes closer to Arnold's scheme, and which may have influenced the Ninth, is Shostakovich's final Symphony (No. 15 (1971)).

In the Fifth Symphony, the home key is E minor. D major is the key of the slow movement, revisited moments before the ending of the finale, and Bb major is the key of much of the finale. Here, Bb minor is the key of the third movement, a key hardly touched upon elsewhere; E minor is the key of the second movement and much of the finale. There is a strong gravitational pull towards E minor in the first movement.

The first movement is marked *Vivace*. It opens with an airy 3/4 theme (the time signature for the whole movement) that glitters with the colouring of harp and glockenspiel added to violins and upper woodwind:

Ex. 9a (opening)

The simple triadic harmony and expressive turns of the opening bars prove deceptive. A level of tonal/harmonic ambiguity sets in as the composer veers towards E minor. The texture is almost entirely two-part counterpoint, save for one passage of simple three-part writing. The dynamic remains at *forte* though the scoring is light. The triadic motif is not developed. Arnold picks up one figure after another in a chain formation that leads to a syncopated passage that is taken over by high trumpets and tuba in four-part harmony. The opening section lasts 53 bars and ends in B minor. We hear the whole section again at the end of the movement, starting at bar 449 and extended by a coda that forces the music to a tonic resolution. The reprise is played *fortissimo*, at half-speed, and is more fully scored. It might therefore be reasonably termed as a *ritornello*, though the listener cannot perceive this until the end of the movement. The reference to concerto form is apt because the central 395 bars of the movement are a series of soloistic episodes – never rising to more than two rhythmically independent parts, and very thinly scored – which follow on from the syncopated passage and explore the material of the opening in many directions. There is some cross-reference between these 'panels' but no obvious sense of formal structure. Despite the lack of rhythmic drive inherent in the material (except perhaps for the widespread use of syncopation), the music is playful; its breeziness only occasionally disturbed by dissonance and tonal non-sequiturs. Much use is made of the harmonic tension created by lines moving by step in contrary motion. Indeed the reprise of Ex. 9a is heralded by nothing more than twenty bars of dotted minim flute dyads, which slow down the pace, paving the way for a four-bar crescendo on the tonic note, scored for brass and timpani. Yet, in defiance of anything that can be explained or justified through musical analysis, the reprise seems inevitable at that point. It rounds off a movement that is unlike anything in Arnold's (or anyone else's) symphonic oeuvre, and far removed from the momentous opening movements of the Ninths of Beethoven, Bruckner, Mahler and any other of the 'greats' of symphonic literature.

The second movement is marked *Allegretto* and is in 9/8 time. Written almost entirely in single-line melody and two-part counterpoint, the movement is based on this E minor theme alone, introduced by solo bassoon:

Ex. 9b

It is one of the composer's most haunting themes; its simplicity reliant on the octave descent and resolution of modal ambiguity via the F# used at the cadence point. The following table outlines the form of the movement:

Bar	Musical material	Scoring (theme)	Scoring (countermelodies)
1	Theme	Bassoon	
9	Theme + 4 bar codetta 1st counter-melody	Bassoon	Flute
21	Theme 2nd counter-melody	Piccolo	Cellos/basses
29	Theme in canon	Strings (lower strings lead)	
38	Theme plus 3rd counter-melody	Oboe	Lower strings
46	First variation	Strings (2 part for 4 bars, then unison, with brass taking over counterpoint)	
54	Theme plus 4th counter-melody	Flute	Bassoon
62	Second variation (based on 4th counter-melody)	Flute/bassoon in octaves	
70	Theme + 4 bar codetta 1st counter-melody	Cellos/violas	Violins
83	Theme 2nd counter-melody	Violins	Lower strings
90	Third variation + 4 bar codetta	Clarinet/horn	
102	Fourth variation (12 bars)	Flute/bassoon	
114	Fifth variation (11 bars)	Trumpet/tuba + harp	
125	Theme + 3 bar codetta 2nd counter-melody	Violins	Lower strings
136	Fifth variation (11 bars) (repeats bars 114 – 124)	Trumpet/tuba + harp	
147	Sixth variation	Piccolo/cellos and basses	
158	Theme	Clarinets/bassoons/ horns/violas/cellos	
166	Theme + 4 bar codetta 1st counter-melody (bars 9 – 20 repeated)	Bassoon	Flute
178	Theme 2nd counter-melody	Oboe	Cellos/basses

	(bars 21 – 28 repeated with different scoring)		
186	Theme in canon (bars 29 – 37 repeated)	Strings (lower strings lead)	
195	Second variation (bars 62 – 69 repeated)	Flute/bassoon in octaves	
203	Theme 2nd countermelody (bars 83 – 89 repeated)	Violins	Lower strings
211	First variation (bars 46 – 53 repeated)	Strings (2-part for 4 bars, then unison, with brass taking over counterpoint)	
219	Theme 2nd countermelody (bars 21 – 28 repeated)	Piccolo	Cellos/basses
227	Third variation + 4-bar codetta (bars 90 – 101 repeated)	Clarinet/horn	
239 - 247	Theme (bars 1 – 8 repeated; final note held for an extra bar)	Bassoon (harp colours 1st note)	

It is interesting to compare this movement with the slow movement of Symphony No 3, which is in the same key. Both structures fall somewhere between the headings 'passacaglia' and 'variation'. The recurring final cadence on E creates a sense of something claustrophobic. In the Third Symphony the accumulation of E minor cadences becomes ever more harrowing. Here they serve to emphasise the sense of solitude, an effect enhanced by use of exact repetition (something that Arnold avoided in the preceding symphonies[58]) and the severity of the modal idiom, which is rarely inflected by chromaticism, and only then in the context of a non-modulating tonal scheme. In this movement Arnold makes many repetitions of a short theme viable by displacing the eight-bar 'loop' with short extensions at strategic points. In the Third Symphony there are many *forte* passages, though they do not occur in a pattern that suggests a clear emotional narrative. Here the only *forte* passages are in the fifth variation, which frames the most richly scored statement of the theme, creating some sort of centre to the movement. The repetitions which follow therefore

[58] An exception being the closing pages of the Sixth

suggest a loose ternary structure, though it is not comparable to the subtle palindromic schemes of the comparable middle movements of the earlier symphonies.

The start of the third movement – *Giubiloso* – is perhaps the only echo of anything from earlier in the cycle[59]; a brisk rhythmic fanfare in Bb minor for trumpets and trombones (X), which launches an invigorating theme whose head-motif (Y) is a motific link to other themes in the movement:

Ex. 9c

Young composers might be intrigued to learn from Arnold how to create the impression of a full-orchestral sound-world from such minimal texture through brilliantly incisive scoring. Was the tempo marking and opening figure a distant memory of the final dance of the second set of English Dances perhaps? As elsewhere, the writing is mainly two-part, with some rhythmically simple chordal passages and instrumental solos. Despite such minimal compositional resources, it is powerful, vigorous and sustains attention. The implications of the marking *giubiloso* also suggest a possible parallel with Tchaikovsky's exultant third movement in the Pathetique Symphony. Yet it is hard to hear this music as anything other than a menacing interlude, at odds with the rest of the symphony, yet a perfect foil for the finale. The intervallic expansion of fig. Y provides the raw material of a number of variants and small developments, such as these[60]:

[59] For instance, the opening of the finales of Nos 2 and 6.
[60] Note the intervallic expansion of Y (Ex.9c)

Ex. 9d

Ex. 9e

And finally, this theme, reminiscent of the rondo theme of the finale of Symphony No 7, which occurs near the mid-point of the movement and loosely corresponds to a Trio section:

Ex. 9f

If the scheme is Scherzo – Trio – Scherzo, then one may not reasonably baulk at the long stretches of music repeated exactly or with small changes from the opening section. An Eighteenth or Nineteenth-Century composer would simply have used the marking *do capo*. The problem is that this is a symphony by a master of subtle change and transformation. We are entitled to feel disappointed.

With a short coda Arnold clears the stage for the twenty-five minute *Lento;* a barren landscape punctuated by a ritornello theme that speaks in a universal tonal language of inescapable loneliness and despair:

Ex. 9g

The wide dynamic range and rich orchestral doublings bring to mind late Bruckner (though this may be coincidental). The sighing fall of the main phrase is rich in historical association. Note also the implied E minor tonality at the start. The home key of the movement (D major) will not be defined until the closing bars, and when it is, it is as unexpected as is the E minor dénouement of the Fifth.

The opening paragraph comes to rest on a low C# – a point of total inertia that precedes the reprise of Ex. 9g. The second main phrase opens on an equally potent rising major-seventh chord, undermined almost at once by the harmonic shift in the bass:

Ex. 9h

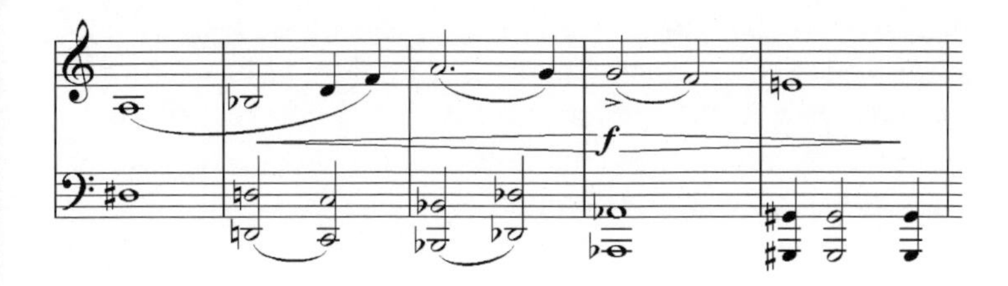

Just before it we reach the first of many exposed tritones and this bleak, funereal rhythm:

Ex. 9i

The rhythmic counterpoint in the movement never goes beyond two-parts, though the enrichment of the lower part by two and three-part harmony brings some respite from the barrenness of the musical landscape. A tiny speck of new figuration at bar 104, faintly reminiscent of Shostakovich,[61] provides a false trail towards a different musical character:

Ex 9j

A brief exchange between trumpet and horn, set against sustained strings, which has 'last post' connotations, frames the second statement of the ritornello, replicating the first fifty-one bars of the movement but without the richly grained sound of woodwind and horn doublings. After a variant of the second phrase (Ex. 9h), a long, virtually a-thematic passage unfolds towards the climax of the movement. Scored only for brass and lower strings, it reaches a *fortissimo* climax, passing through many tonal centres before settling on a bright E major seventh chord. A quiet 'duo' for violas and cellos settles on a low octave E, reinforcing the feeling that we have reached the key centre of the movement. The final statement of the ritornello ensues at bar 303, further reduced in scoring and halted after eighteen bars on the low C#, which acts as a leading note to the final D major chord, marked *pianissimo* and scored across six octaves for almost the whole orchestra. A radiant ending then – the chord a redemptive symbol? Not according to Malcolm Arnold, who in a recorded interview with conductor Andrew Penny, accepts Penny's suggestion that the movement is a "complete surrender to despair" adding that it was "entirely meant, even with the D major ending."[62] Paul R.W. Jackson[63] has pointed out Arnold's conflicting statements about the work, and suggests that the security created by the work's dedicatee is expressed here. It's certainly true that without Anthony Day the work would not have come into being, but for my part, Arnold's statement in conversation with Andrew Penny

---

[61] Specifically, the accompaniment to the second subject of the first movement of Symphony no 5.

[62] Interview recorded for Naxos CD 8.553526.

[63] Paul R.W. Jackson: *The Life and Music of Sir Malcolm Arnold.*

rings true. D major is the home key but almost the entire movement denies it, making the sudden shift to the tonic an empty gesture; the only touch of Arnoldian irony in a work that speaks plainly and from the heart.

Arnold described the Ninth as "an amalgam of all my knowledge of humanity."[64] The listener must judge whether or not the composer realised his aim. I suspect that few admirers of the cycle will see the Ninth as a fitting conclusion. The music does not live up to the level of compositional invention of its predecessors. Yet, in its own way, and for different reasons, it ranks alongside Symphony No. 7 as one of the most moving symphonies of the cycle. We hear Arnold's voice in the plainest terms. It is, for all of its flaws, the work of a master craftsman who, even when firing on less than his full quota of cylinders, wrote music that is far more than the sum of its notes.

Conclusions

The British love of symphonic music can be seen in orchestral concert programmes at both amateur and professional level. Symphonic repertoire, it seems, still holds pride of place despite the extraordinary diversity of new music. Why then is it that no symphonic cycle by a British composer born after Walton[65] has gained a secure foothold in the regular UK concert repertoire, yet some British symphonists of that period are represented by one or more complete recorded cycles? Indeed, in the case of Arnold, the Decca *Complete Edition* set of the Eleven Symphonies, issued as a limited edition and no longer available, is currently a collector's item selling at premium prices on the internet. If we go back to an earlier period, Bax – an equally neglected symphonic composer – is also well represented on CD with the same number (three[66]) of complete recorded cycles of his symphonies as Arnold, yet they are seldom, if ever, performed live.

If the answer is that none of these symphonists has an international profile, the counter arguments are:

[64] Interview with Andrew Penny recorded for Naxos CD 8.553526.
[65] In the case of composers born within the latter part of this period, it may be too early to say that they will not gain a foothold, and there are some high-profile figures such as James MacMillan.
[66] Three under one conductor, but more than three recordings of each work.

- That amongst the 'repertoire' British symphonists - Elgar, Vaughan Williams and Walton – the symphonies of Vaughan Williams in particular have made only limited headway outside these shores.

- It is less likely that composers such as Tippett, Rawsthorne, Simpson, Arnold and <u>many</u> others will be taken up internationally if they are not first championed here. Recognition at home is usually a springboard for the wider dissemination of repertoire.

A stronger argument is that there is simply too much British symphonic music of real stature to be accommodated – the 'where do we start?' attitude. But there is another factor, which I've alluded to, and which is covered in depth in the major studies on Arnold. It concerns the backlash against tonal music, particularly during the 1960's, which targeted the tradition of highlighting symphonic music at the Cheltenham Festival and chose Arnold for its most savage attack. The direction that Arnold took after the Fifth Symphony was likely to be problematic for his admirers and was seized upon by his detractors at a time when rumours of his mental illness were beginning to circulate beyond a small circle, and as we know, the direction in which this unfolded culminated in the shocked reaction to the Ninth.

The extent to which Arnold's mental illness has a bearing on his achievement as a symphonist is complex and sensitive. My views are:

1. That having re-read *Malcolm Arnold Rogue Genius* by Anthony Meredith and Paul Harris just before studying the complete cycle, I knew the sometimes tragic background to each work but was amazed to find how little correlation there was between the composer's state of health and personal circumstances at the time, and the quality of each work. Indeed the Sixth – the only work that I find uneven – was written during one of Arnold's happiest and most settled periods. The Ninth is a special case but it is the work of a disabled composer, not a disordered one.

2. The 'highs' and 'lows' that we experience in works such as the Third Symphony are deeply felt in Arnold's oeuvre, just as they are in the works of Tchaikovsky, Bruckner, Mahler and others. They are part of the artist; therefore it is pointless to speculate on the type of music

that Arnold might have written had he not suffered from a condition that would these days most likely be termed 'bipolar'.

3. Arnold's symphonic cycle is slightly uneven, but that in itself is not *de facto* evidence that mental illness impaired his work. If Shostakovich had written only the Second, Third and Twelfth Symphonies, he would probably not be seen as a major symphonist. All things considered, the quality of the Nine is remarkably consistent and not just because Arnold was a master craftsman. In my view, the first four of Arnold's Symphonies are masterly works of unflagging concentration and invention. In the Fifth he raises his game to a level that places him in the front rank of British symphonists and lays claim to international stature. Each of the remaining four breaks fresh ground and widens the scope of the cycle, with varying degrees of success. The Seventh represents a scale of ambition beyond anything that went before it and offers the most intense experience of the canon. If I find it less satisfying than the Fifth, it is because I place the level of clearly audible integration carried through in the Fifth and its effectiveness in clinching the musical journey at a premium, but I recognise that the depth of feeling in the later symphonies is at times even greater than in the Fifth, and that the Seventh in particular has an unfettered quality. And I should add that with every hearing, there are new discoveries in each work.

At the start of this paper I put forward various ways of categorising Arnold's symphonic writing as a means of approaching the music. I've tried to outline some of the ways in which Arnold presents a coherent tonal symphony and the subtlety with which he handles traditional forms. The elements that confound and confuse listeners are part of Arnold's makeup as an artist. For me the 'unidentifiable programmatic elements' account in large part for the fascination of these works. Arnold was right to draw a line - in his programme notes – beyond which the listener is left to find their own responses.

Amongst Malcolm Arnold's many gifts as a composer, the ability to write functional tonal music without the baggage of post-Wagnerian styles, and make it sound fresh and modern lies at the heart of his achievement. By 'modern', I do not suggest that Arnold reinvented or replaced the tonal system, but he somehow infused it with a kind of freshness that more conservative composers of his day were not gifted enough to achieve, hence the term 'modern' as opposed to 'old-fashioned' or 'conservative'. Now that the ideological battles of Arnold's time have receded, it is possible to hear this music afresh for what it is. It isn't good enough to dismiss the music as conservative or even 'irrelevant' simply because the composer's language includes triadic harmony. Besides, as I've attempted to illustrate, the handling of tonality and tonal structures is not merely second-hand. Where Arnold turns to serial technique, he absorbs it into his compositional armoury and broadens his language without compromising his creative vision. 'The Nine' sound remarkably fresh. They are, in my view, of their time but not ahead of it except in so far as they anticipate the poly-stylism of some later symphonic composers. Most importantly, Arnold's language is exceptionally rich in the terms of the power of association, without descending into pastiche. In his preface to the Novello revised (2000) edition of the Fifth Symphony, Millan Sachania describes the dominant thirteenth chord that ushers in the return of the slow movement's main theme as 'an aural quotation mark'. The phrase 'aural quotation mark' could be applied not only to the big gestures such as the one that Sachania describes, but to a wealth of small detail across the whole cycle. The gift of aural association served Arnold well as a film composer and lies at the heart of Arnold's musical language. It is original music loaded with meaning, expressed in a way that engages with the ordinary listeners' musical experience (including modern 'vernacular' music as well as 'classical' styles) conveyed in a complex and fascinating way that connects with the listener's expectations of musical form and structure but goes its own way. The composer takes ownership of the language of the past and present, makes it his own, and with it, explores the challenge of the symphony. The results, at their best, are explosive.

Timothy Bowers
May 2011

Appendix:
Symphony no 5 - Finale
Analysis of pitch content, Voice-leading, motific content and dynamics

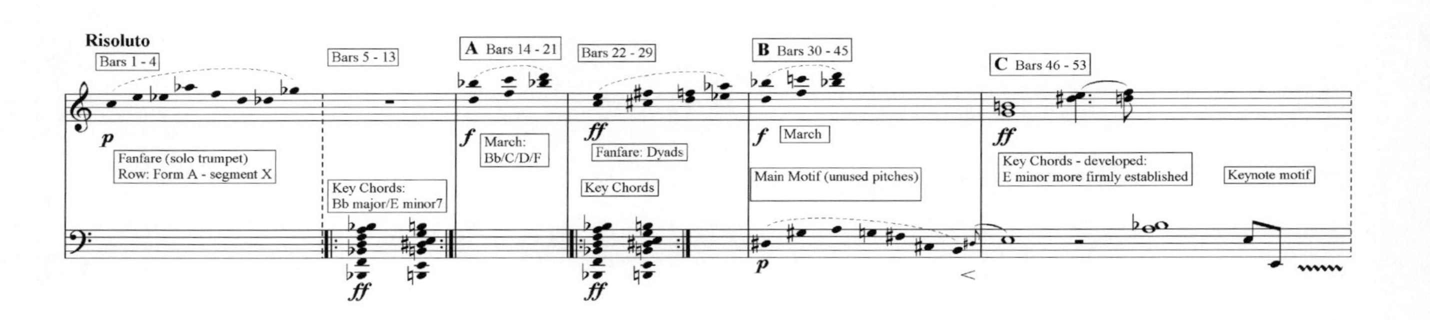

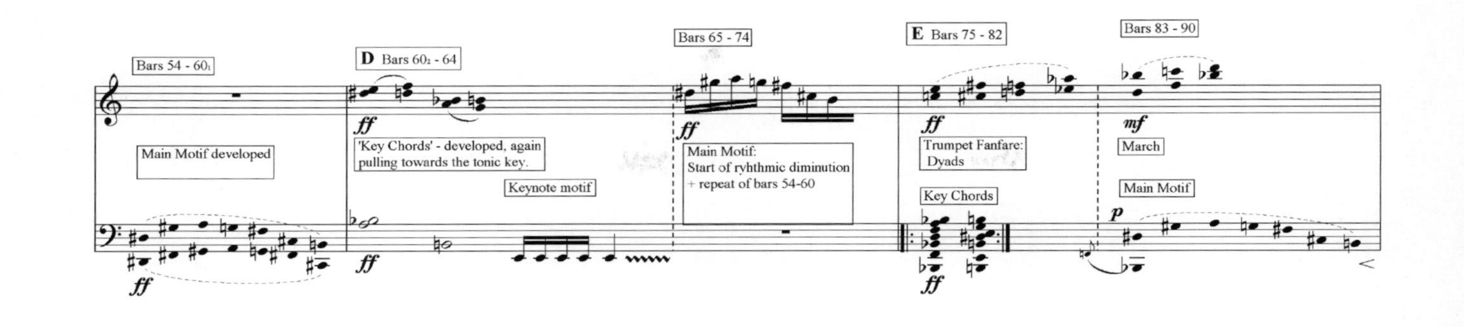

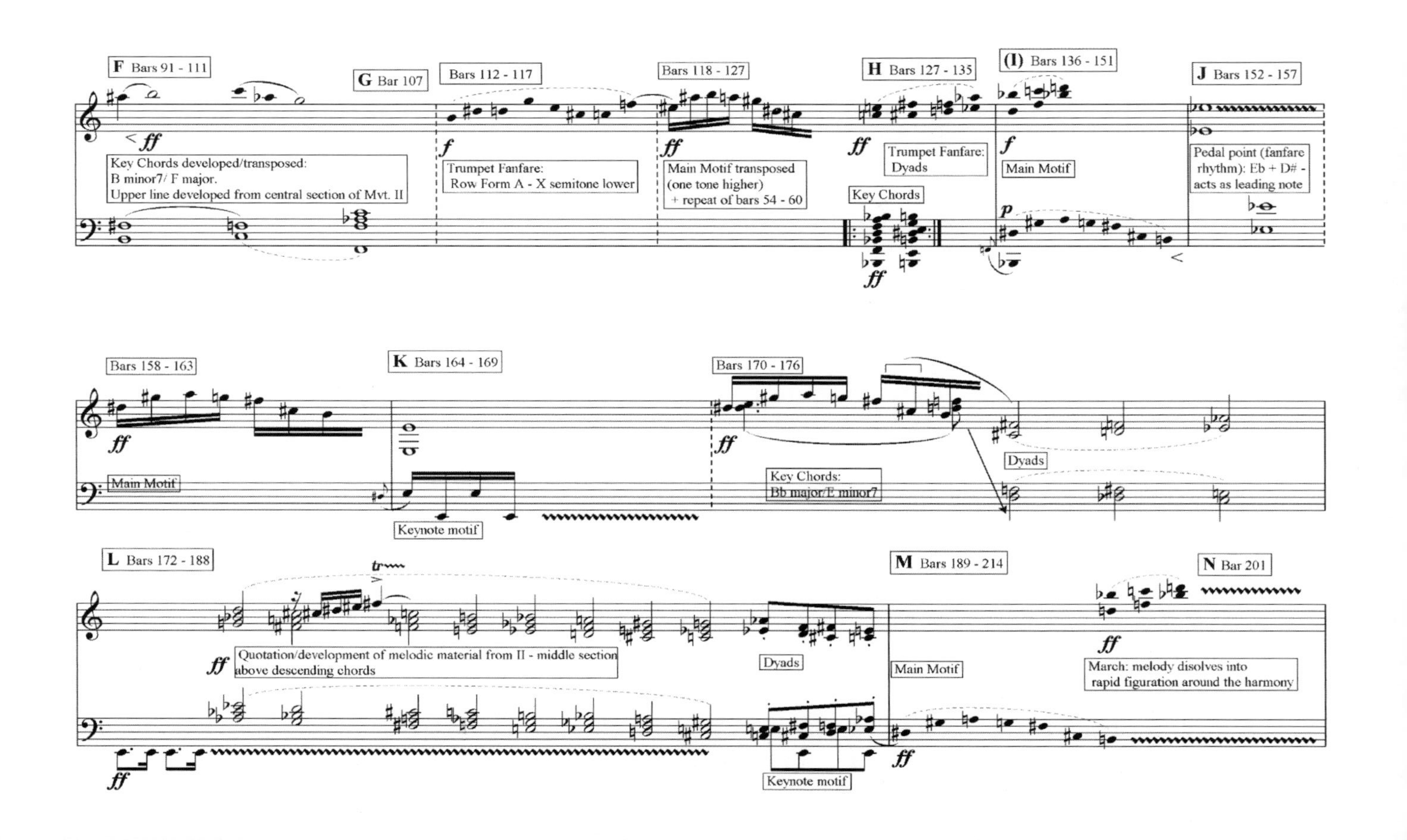
F Bars 91 - 111
G Bar 107
Bars 112 - 117
Bars 118 - 127
H Bars 127 - 135
(I) Bars 136 - 151
J Bars 152 - 157
Key Chords developed/transposed:
B minor7/ F major.
Upper line developed from central section of Mvt. II
Trumpet Fanfare:
Row Form A - X semitone lower
Main Motif transposed
(one tone higher)
+ repeat of bars 54 - 60
Trumpet Fanfare:
Dyads
Key Chords
Main Motif
Pedal point (fanfare
rhythm): Eb + D# -
acts as leading note
Bars 158 - 163
K Bars 164 - 169
Bars 170 - 176
Main Motif
Keynote motif
Key Chords:
Bb major/E minor7
Dyads
L Bars 172 - 188
M Bars 189 - 214
N Bar 201
Quotation/development of melodic material from II - middle section
above descending chords
Dyads
Keynote motif
Main Motif
March: melody disolves into
rapid figuration around the harmony

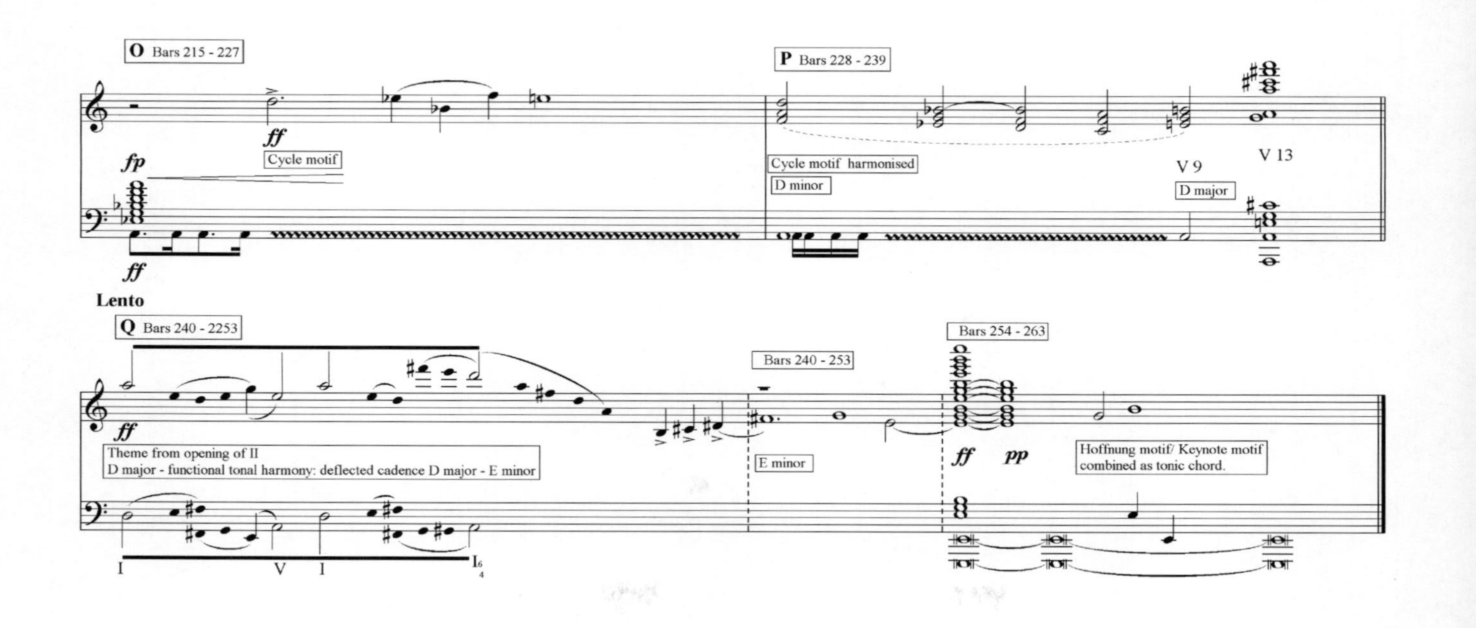
O Bars 215 - 227
fp
ff
Cycle motif
ff
P Bars 228 - 239
Cycle motif harmonised
D minor
V 9
D major
V 13
Lento
Q Bars 240 - 2253
ff
Theme from opening of II
D major - functional tonal harmony: deflected cadence D major - E minor
I
V
I
I 6 4
Bars 240 - 253
E minor
Bars 254 - 263
ff
pp
Hoffnung motif/ Keynote motif
combined as tonic chord.

Comments:

1. Pitch content:

The pitch content of the Fanfare and March sections of the movement is restricted to the formations given above. At letters **L** and **Q** Arnold quotes from the second movement. Both passages are tonal. At **L** the opening of the upper line and its harmonic support are shown. The functional tonal harmony of the theme at **Q** is represented by reductive analysis.

2. Voice leading:

The serial and tonal music interacts in the following ways:

- The March is in Bb. Unused pitches form the main motif of the movement, minus the keynote E, which acts as a pivot.
- The Fanfare uses form A segment X of the Prime (row). The Fanfare rhythm is applied to the dyads. These elements interact with the 'key chords' motif which juxtaposes the two main keys of the movement (Bb major (march key)/E minor (home key).
- Pedal points on E (tonic) and A (dominant of D) anchor those keys and are prepared by the choice of non-tonal pitch material in the preceding bars.
- Symbols such as slurs, arrows and lines show the voice-leading between sections based on different pitch material.

3. Motific content:

The movement uses all of the main motifs of the Symphony, plus the row (prime), and quotes from the A and C sections of the slow movement. The March and 'main motif' are the only fresh material.

4. Dynamics:

The dynamic changes and contrasts in the movement are used to highlight some aspects of the structure. The 'main motif' is initially heard at low dynamic levels. As it becomes louder, the March dissolves into rapid figuration.

NB Letter I is omitted from the sequence of rehearsal marks in the Novello score. I have used it (bracketed) to denote a clear point of demarcation (return of the March theme).

Bibliography

Burton-Page, Piers (1994) *Philharmonic Concerto* Methuen
Cole, Hugo (1989) *Malcolm Arnold An Introduction to his Music* Faber and Faber
Jackson, Paul R.W. (2003) *The Life and Music of Malcolm Arnold* Ashgate
Meredith, Anthony and Harris, Paul (2004) *Malcolm Arnold; Rogue Genius* Thames /Elkin
Mitchell, Donald 1995) *Cradles of the New* Faber and Faber
Sachania, Millania (2000) *Malcolm Arnold Symphony No 5 (preface)* Novello
Schafer, R.M. (1963) *British Composers in Interview* Faber and Faber
Thöne, Raphael D. (2007) *Malcolm Arnold A Composer of Real Music* edition Wissenschaft

Acknowledgements:

I am grateful to the following colleagues at the Royal Academy of Music for their interest and advice in preparing this chapter:

Christopher Austin
Paul Harris
Nicholas Walker

Jude Carlton

I think it safe to say that the composers writing here would all argue that the symphonies of Malcolm Arnold are generally unappreciated by listeners and composers alike. It is perhaps my own generation, though, that appreciates his cycle the least. There is, among my contemporaries, a distrust, even a fear, surrounding the idea of 'the symphony', which may go some way in explaining the lack of warmth towards the symphonies of Arnold as well as those by the other great British symphonist of the second half of the twentieth century – Robert Simpson. I cannot pretend to be unaffected by this cultural phenomenon – it is unlikely that I will write a work called 'symphony' (the word, for me, simply carries with it too much baggage). However, there is absolutely no sense in ignoring works simply because they go by a name that you yourself are scared of. We miss out on an awful lot if we forget Arnold's symphonies – there is much to learn from his intriguing and multi-faceted cycle.

I am lucky that for many of my teenage years I was taught composition by one of Arnold's biographers, Paul Harris. Inevitably, the symphonies of Arnold were given a justified emphasis amongst the great array of works that Paul introduced me to. As something of a sponge, I was, as a 13/14 year-old, quite directly influenced by the foreground sonority of these symphonies. Arnold's appropriation of jazz into his musical language appealed greatly and I began to emulate this aspect of his style. Associated with his importing of jazz into the symphony is his habit of juxtaposing styles or genres – a feature of his music that had a great emotional impact on me as a teenager, but an aspect whose significance I did not fully comprehend at the time. Of course, the juxtaposition of genres was not Arnold's idea. There is a long history of mixing music, a history which perhaps reaches a climax with the symphonies of Mahler. As Jim Samson notes, in Mahler, the 'guest' genre often threatens to overthrow the supremacy of the 'host' genre.

Shamefully, when I first heard, as a 14-year-old, Arnold's most dramatic genetic hybrid – the second movement of his Sixth Symphony, I had not yet become properly acquainted with the works of Mahler. As a result, Arnold's remarkable juxtaposition here of funeral march and Sixties psychedelia made all the more impact. I now perceive the parallels between this movement and perhaps the third movement of Mahler's First

Symphony with its unnerving combination of funeral march and Klezmer music, but it was Arnold's work which first demonstrated to me the expressive potential of bringing together seemingly incompatible music.

I think it usual that as young composers mature they become more self-conscious of their influences. In retrospect, I can see that this was the case for me – the jazz influence via Arnold became less important, as did the playing with different styles. This is an inevitable part of developing as a composer – though the rejection of the influence is usually less thorough than we perceive it to be. I cannot personally assess if and how Arnold's symphonies influence my work now, but often, early compositional influences remain integral to the background of a composer's music without the realisation of it.

There is one aspect of Arnold's symphonies that I now understand as something of great worth. Although the cycle has its dark moments, most notably in the Ninth Symphony, the darkness is almost always balanced by a brightness and often a disregard for the perceived seriousness of the genre. A prime example is provided by the finale of the Sixth Symphony with its raucous two-fingered salute. This salute is I think directed to the musical establishment of the Sixties with its general disregard for all things which were not *avant garde*. Though the importance of continental musical developments at this time cannot be denied, within this context Arnold's sense of lightness and of fun come as a truly refreshing breath of fresh air.

I admit that I have only quite recently realised the importance of 'lightness' in music and in art in general. This has stemmed from reading the work of Italo Calvino who is a master of balancing a lightness of touch with a deep profundity – a balance which is perhaps most akin musically to the classical aesthetic. Arnold probably never read any Calvino, but he too is brilliant at displaying lightness without compromising his ability to make important statements. The lightness demonstrates, I feel, a generosity of spirit, and an unselfishness which is admirable. This is the aspect of Arnold's symphonies as well as his other music that I now see as most valuable – against the tide. Arnold's largely generous and bright works, even in times of turmoil, reveal a great warmth as well as a wicked sense of humour. A general refusal to get weighed down by current musical trends as well as ones own psychological state (though he occasionally gave into this) is an attitude that is commendable and one that I hope to cultivate myself in the future.

Edward Gregson

Arnold the symphonist: An appreciation

One of the historical truisms about classical music is that composers tend to go in and out of fashion. That is no less true today than in the past. If we look at the twentieth century alone there are numerous examples. Witness the dark clouds (albeit short lived) that descended on the music of both Sibelius and Vaughan Williams, to name but two, after their deaths (which happened to be within a year of each other). Gratifyingly, both have re-emerged with perhaps even greater reputations than when they were alive. In the case of Sibelius in particular, his cycle of seven symphonies is now recognised as one of the most important in the history of the genre. Whereas in the case of say Schoenberg, the revolutionary *par excellence*, whilst his compositional theories remain important, his music is performed less now than ever before. Why? Well, perhaps he just wasn't a great composer; or perhaps his theories chained him up too much. In any case, the comparison with his pupil Alban Berg is fascinating – his star has risen increasingly over the years, maybe because he composed some of the most memorable scores of the last century, where theory was not allowed to suppress natural inspiration. The world would certainly be a poorer place without his violin concerto, or his opera *Wozzeck*, to name but two of his masterpieces.

When we consider Malcolm Arnold's contribution to English musical life we realise that whilst his more serious works (i.e. his symphony cycle) might well have suffered from the same fate as others, certain works in his output are alive and well, and probably always will be. As I write this article, his set of *English Dances* is receiving yet another outing on BBC Radio 3, and that is surely one of Arnold's problems, or perhaps not his problem but ours! As a melodist and orchestrator he is up there among the greatest (Tchaikovsky, eat your heart out – well almost!), mainly because he had a natural gift for melodic invention which others might strive for but never quite manage. One of the best examples of this gift can be seen in his film music and ballets where melodic invention is of the essence, illuminating the visual landscape, often without us knowing it. Once again, Tchaikovsky immediately springs to mind. Indeed, it could also be said that in the case of Tchaikovsky, his symphonies have always courted divided critical comment, for example, that his thematic material is too self-contained, not ripe for development, and so on.

The British symphony, almost a genre type in its own right, had a notable presence in twentieth century British music before its decline in recent years. After Stanford, Parry, and Elgar, the genre was expanded by Vaughan Williams, Rubbra, Walton, and Tippett, before Arnold's generation, via the 'Cheltenham symphony' years, explored new pathways with the influence of Sibelius, Nielsen, and Shostakovich, as well as Schoenberg in a few cases, perhaps portraying a more cosmopolitan outlook. Malcolm Arnold was one of the first of these 'new generation' composers to commence his symphonic cycle with his First Symphony, completed in 1949 but not premiered until 1951. This was around the same time as Lennox Berkeley, Alan Rawsthorne, Humphrey Searle, Peter Racine Fricker, Benjamin Frankel, Robert Simpson and Alun Hoddinott, as well as others, started theirs. For me, however, there is none better than the Arnold cycle of nine symphonies, and it is regrettable that they seem to have gone out of fashion, at least for the time being. Having said that, most of Arnold's generation of symphonists have suffered the same fate. It seems that we no longer want to hear them (the 'we' here meaning the musical establishment, whether that means the BBC, orchestral managers, conductors, critics, et al). However, there are many of us who do still want to hear these symphonies performed, and often!

What are the reasons for the demise of the Arnold cycle in particular? Well, the musical establishment has always been deeply suspicious of popularity – somehow 'easy' gratification, in their terms, seems distasteful. But Arnold's music is not like that at all – rather, it is beautifully crafted from a compositional point of view, exquisitely orchestrated, with a melodic gift to die for! This can be heard most readily I suppose in his sets of English, Irish, Scottish, and Cornish Dances. They are beautiful miniatures in the same way as Dvorak's Slavonic Dances, and just as good. No, if you want 'easy' gratification, go to Lloyd Webber (and even then you would be searching for it!). For many people, the music of his Dances is Malcolm Arnold, for they may have never heard a single symphony of his. However, those of us who know and love his symphonies see another side of Arnold, one that is intense, complex, dark; one that is searching for the truth about the human dilemma. He has sometimes been referred to as 'the English Shostakovich' and there is certainly some truth in that, particularly as Shostakovich, for different reasons, was also a troubled soul, grappling with the complexities of life and a totalitarian state, but in so doing produced fifteen symphonies that arguably are the true successors to Mahler's ten, But that particular description of Arnold does not give him the credit he deserves. He is his own man, so to speak, with a strong compositional personality, and a style that is immediately recognisable. True enough, he admired Shostakovich, but his answers to life's problems through music produced different results.

So why is it that Arnold was such a fine symphonist? And what makes his best symphonies so effective in their execution? Well, first and foremost it is the quality of the ideas themselves – the invention of material that is both ripe for developmental processes but also, when required, self-contained enough to satisfy his need for emotional expression. This can be heard in many of his slow movements where the shadow of Mahler is omnipresent. Long expressive lines of melody are woven through a telling harmonic palette, with a contrapuntal control of which Mahler would have approved. The similarities with Mahler do not end there. No-one could possibly call Mahler a purist – and neither was Arnold. The idea of the symphony needing to embrace and express the whole world, in both its physical (i.e. the natural world), and personal/intellectual manifestations, with all the resulting contradictions and complexities, was of course Mahler's mantra, and is something that Arnold certainly inherited (as indeed did Shostakovich). Thus, we do not get 'pure', 'intellectually sealed' symphonies in the way that perhaps Rubbra, Searle, or Simpson sought; rather, we get a whole range of musical landscapes within the symphonic structure – one minute a tightly organised symphonic Allegro, the next a military march, here a sardonic Scherzo, there a deeply felt, emotionally-charged Adagio, and for good measure a fugal Finale (eg the 1st and 4th symphonies).

The 1st Symphony sets out Arnold's view of the genre very effectively. The first movement is developed from the opening three note motif, with fragmented gestures seemingly fighting one another for dominance. There are some similarities with Nielsen's 5th Symphony in this regard, not least in the repetitive minor 3rd ostinati and pedals which permeate the movement. The second movement starts off rather like a Mahler middle movement *ländler*, seemingly there to release some of the tension from the first movement, but it soon develops a darker tone, as Arnold's slow movements mostly do. There is no resolution here, despite the tranquil C major ending. The final movement delights in contrapuntal bravura, with the composer showing his prowess not only in the process of note manipulation (note the Bachian device of the inversion of the fugue subject at the halfway point), but also in the way he exercises total control of the orchestra. His years spent in the trumpet section of the London Philharmonic Orchestra clearly gave him a mastery of orchestration that defines his music in a highly individual way.

The 2nd Symphony has always been one of the most frequently performed of the canon, and it is not hard to see why. The themes here are more 'outward facing', more clearly defined, and it has four movements which are beautifully contrasted in their closed-form characterisation. Also, in this symphony, the Shostakovich-inspired scherzo makes its first appearance to telling effect. Then, we descend into a world of personal introspection with a quasi-Mahlerian funeral march which surely contains the first echoes of Arnold's deepening personal problems. However, the final movement throws these worries aside with typically Arnold 'con brio' – no hint of darkness here, just general good spirits and a sense of fun!

The 3rd and 4th symphonies both make significant steps in the process of the maturing of Arnold's symphonic language. There is an expansion in the means of expressive intent, particularly in the first movement of the 4th where 'urban cool' (passages under the influence of Bernstein's 'mambo' music in *West Side Story*) enters his compositional toolbox for the first time. Although the movement starts conventionally enough, already in the first six bars we detect something different with the added textures of bongos and marimba. Add to this other 'exotic' percussion instruments, plus harp and celesta, and you have an entirely new palette of orchestral colours which he exploits to maximum effect. Unsurprisingly for Arnold, in this first movement, the 'urban cool' is contrasted with a second subject of jaw-dropping diatonic simplicity (you might call it a damn good tune), which if anything he overdoes in its repetitive sequencing.

The fact that this particular symphony was commissioned by William Glock and the BBC, and premiered at the Royal Festival Hall with Arnold himself conducting, may be surprising in itself, but it may also give a clue as to why this symphony came out as it did. There may have been a typical Arnold 'naughtiness' in wanting to surprise the musical establishment, for no-one quite expected the work they got! It is both irreverent and surprisingly original. Who would have expected the Ivesian tritonal *Alla Marcia* episode in the final movement, after the opening fugue, itself reminiscent of Britten from his *Young Person's Guide*? Arnold describes this moment as 'going crazy', which indeed it does! The symphony is a *tour de force*, and for this writer anyway, certainly one his most original achievements.

In enthusing about the 4th, I do not wish to side-step the 3rd which has one of the most heart-searching (and longest) slow movements of the cycle. It is music of great intensity and sincerity, and the fact that Arnold chooses to reference Shostakovich's personal musical cipher (DSCH) within his main theme perhaps shows where the inspiration for this music lies; (indeed, he uses the same four note reference, even more so, in the slow movement of the 4th). The tension inherent in the music partially derives from a much more chromatic melodic utterance than is the norm in Arnold's music. In addition, the flowering counterpoint which delivers these melodic strands adds to the emotional impact of the music. The first movement of the 3rd follows on naturally from the 2nd symphony in its orthodox use of symphonic argument, but it is more expansive than its predecessor and develops its material more comprehensively, contrasting two strongly defined themes in an impressive manner. Once again, the final movement is an Arnold *joie de vivre* and is none the worse for that. In this case, it seems an entirely fitting conclusion to the tensions of the previous movements.

With the 5th and 6th symphonies we reach Arnold's full maturity as a symphonic essayist. Both are compact in form and structure (the 6th more so than the 5th), both full of glorious music, both progressing the 'glittering' textures of the 4th Symphony in their orchestration. Indeed, the first few bars of the 5th open up a new sound-world, unlike anything we have experienced before in his music. This expanded palette also enables him to take the symphonic argument in a different direction, to compelling effect. The long and 'personal' slow movement is a portrait of his first wife (as he once told me), and is intense in its gradual release of emotional intent. But it is not quite the angst-ridden music of the 2nd or 3rd symphonies despite its emotionally-charged middle section climax – no, it is more the serene Mahlerian model of that composer's 5th Symphony *Adagietto* (itself a portrait of his own wife Alma) in its melodic and harmonic simplicity.

If I have a criticism of the 5th it is of its final strands, which in my opinion do not resolve the expectancy created by the first two movements. I can live with the third movement even though it can't quite decide if it wants to inhabit the sardonic world of the Shostakovich scherzo, or the more sugary world of Arnold's Dances, but it is the final movement which I find disappointing, not in its initial musical argument (here Shostakovich's shadow is cast in relation to the contrast between a simple military penny-whistle tune and the angular chromatic outbursts which attempt to destroy it), which is compelling. No, it is the 'easy' and somewhat sentimental route that Arnold takes at the conclusion of the symphony, where he brings back the 'love theme' of the slow movement in what can only be described as a 'Gone with the Wind' moment. The harmonic/tonal progression which leads to this recap can only be described as rather clumsy! He partially retrieves the situation with the final few bars which dissolve into emptiness and despair, as opposed to the Hollywood ending that might have been (perhaps a musical premonition of the impending breakdown of his first marriage?). Nevertheless, such a miscalculation is surprising for a composer who usually makes the right calls!

In a different way to the 4th Symphony, the 6th Symphony is a masterpiece of invention and ideas. The first movement's symphonic argument takes on yet a new direction to the 5th. This is unrelenting music, compulsive in its developmental processes, completely assured in its delivery. The slow movement is a surprise given Arnold's previous slow movements, for it deals in suggestion rather than rhetorical certainty. There are constant changes of emphasis, and an underlying tension that is both disturbing and convincing. If once again the finale doesn't quite live up to expectations (given the scale of the first two movements one might have expected a more 'heroic' finale), it doesn't resort to the rather hollow gesture of the 5th Symphony's ending. All in all, the 6th is a symphony of real substance and durability, and deserves to be heard much more often than it is.

The final three symphonies are something of an enigma. By the time Arnold had completed his 7th Symphony in 1973 he was already starting to suffer from the mental torment that would eventually consume him. If the previous six symphonies presented an external world of conflicting emotions, then these last three symphonies are internal creations. Just as Shostakovich, towards the end of his life, became more and more introspective – witness the stark subject matter and dark musical sonorities of the 14th Symphony, and the enigmatic 15th with its strange 'other-worldly' musical references to Rossini and Wagner – so did Arnold. The music in these symphonies exists in a strange hinterland between dreams and nightmares. Some of the music in the 7th Symphony is truly extraordinary. In particular, the musical landscape of the slow movement has an imagery unlike anything else in Arnold's music. It creates a mood of intense sadness, at least for the present writer. The musical syntax of the final movement has a disconnection which is disturbing. The Celtic music episode exists in a dream-like world, suspended from reality, and the final three climactic F major chords have a hollowness which again seems unrelated to what has come before. All in all, it is an enigma, but is it great music? I can't decide!

Whereas the 8th Symphony is not great music, that's for sure! By now Arnold's mental health was deteriorating. Given that, it is remarkable that the music of the 8th has a viable musical narrative. However, in the opening movement, the extensive use of the Irish marching tune, taken from an earlier film score he had composed, does not make compelling material for a symphonic allegro, despite the imaginative dreamscape he creates for its use. The slow movement employs reduced chamber-like orchestration in a harrowing musical narrative; the overwhelming mood is one of despair and regret. All the more surprising then that the finale reverts to an earlier period of Arnold's consciousness, at least at the opening – the world of his ballet music springs to mind. It is as if he is remembering his earlier musical journeys, summoning up one last joyful commentary as if in a dream (e.g. the main theme's appearance on celesta and tuned percussion sounds just like that). The music takes a slightly tortured route through its musical journey before reaching its (forced?) triumphant ending, and the final unison dominant/tonic cadence could be seen as a tongue-in-cheek gesture, and if so, it wouldn't surprise any of us, for that was part of Malcolm's personality.

As for the 9th Symphony, I do not agree with the final sentence of the booklet notes of the Naxos CD for this work which states: "Arnold's Ninth has a message for us all". If simplicity, even naivety, can work at a symphonic level, then it has to be assured in its control. Gorecki's 3rd Symphony may be one example of this being realised, albeit within a different stylistic world. In Arnold's case, I fear the mind was not in control of the material, and the result is a fractured musical syntax, devoid of any real meaning or substance. When there is so much literal repetition, especially in the long final Lento (likened to Mahler 9 by at least one commentator, but for me far removed from that masterpiece) it is difficult to make coherent sense of the music. A sad note to end on perhaps? Well no, not for me, for a great artist is often flawed in some way, and Arnold's sad demise takes nothing away from the achievements of a lifetime of outstanding creative energy.

In summary, my admiration for Malcolm Arnold's music is immense. He holds a special place in my affections, for as a young composer, the first work of mine to make it onto a commercial LP record (that ages me!) was my Brass Quintet, written when I was student at the Royal Academy of Music. One of the other works on that disc (the Hallé Brass Consort on Pye 'Collector's Label') was Malcolm Arnold's 1st Brass Quintet (the famous one!). That was a work I knew well and probably tried to emulate in my own quintet. A little later, in 1973, I interviewed him for a music magazine (the interview lasting for well over two hours and with more than two bottles of wine!). We discussed many aspects of his musical life including his opinion of music critics ("they have to earn a living"!). He had a tough time with critics, as we know, but he didn't seem to care much about their opinions of his music. He suffered particularly from the negativity of Hans Keller and Peter Heyworth (he rather sarcastically said that he would be happy to pay Peter Heyworth's overdraft any day!), but he was also respected and admired by many others and we should not forget that. Most composers I know respect his music, whatever their own musical personality might be, for the one thing which draws a composer's admiration is compositional craft, and Arnold had that in abundance. Many composers would be jealous of a compositional technique such as his, let alone his remarkable fluency and apparent ease with the creative process.

As for his cycle of nine symphonies – well, it stands out as being one of the most distinguished by any British composer after the Second World War. We should clamour to bring his symphonies to the concert platform more often. They are enduring and memorable works by a great creative mind, and we should rejoice in their existence.

Kenneth Hesketh

The Nine - a personal perspective

As a young composer I came to Malcolm Arnold's music through the ever-popular Dance suites, overtures, the *Little Suite* for brass and some of the chamber music. When I subsequently came across the symphonies they forced me to reassess his work as they revealed a composer capable of a much greater range of musical expression. Today, I find myself both perplexed and intrigued by Arnold's complete symphonic worldview, and though one shouldn't determine the man by the music, the composer's turbulent life seems reflected in the symphonies from start to finish.

When, as a young composer myself, I encountered the First Symphony, it left me a little unsure as to its intent; *schizophrenic* seemed a fair appraisal! However, it is a work that points to Arnold's mature voice, already showing many of the composer's trademark features. Harmonically, I still retain a fondness for it, possibly because the approach to dissonance is so quirky, turbulent, even unpredictable. As for its overall form, it is equally volatile, yet taken as a whole, the symphony's sheer power and affable personality remain infectious.

The Second is an altogether more assured work in my opinion, and the strong melodic influences of Britten, and Tippett in particular, have started to dissipate. The melodic gift, both serious and cheeky (viz. Hobson's Choice 'jaunty'), seem fully assured. The dark and militaristic scherzo (surely the precursor to its equivalent in the 5th Symphony) tears along with irresistible verve. Colours of the eerie slow movement and more energetic final movement from the *Cornish Dances* emerge in movement III, whilst the last movement, the stuff of the *English Dances* surely, has some special colouristic moments (upper string harmonic glissandi for example, these being quite unusual in Arnold's output as a whole). Shades of Shostakovich (the 9th from 1945) occasionally peek through, but I still feel that it really is in this symphony that Arnold's most accustomed colours come through strongly and persuasively.

For me, the Third, whilst being structurally more advanced and harmonically assured than its predecessors, comes across as a little too facile. Beautifully scored and carefully constructed from a symphonic point of view, it somehow never really takes off, possibly because it's almost too text-book (the ending of the symphony itself is a good example of what I mean!). The one movement that does leave a rather haunting impression is the *Lento* second movement. Full of subtle harmonic shifts that are not quite yet the standard cycle one associates with the composer, the melodic writing emanates out of the underlying chord progression, with many harmonically tense collisions in the interweaving counterpoint. The weighty and fraught atmosphere at the climax is certainly striking (worthy of Shostakovich at his best), and its proportions and length are impressive.

The Fourth is an intriguing work, despite the somewhat 'filmy' feel to the opening movement (the sort of music that might underscore a moody thriller or American film noir!). There are some wonderful orchestral moments in the *Scherzo* and *Andantino* movements which are true Arnold. The use of palindromes in his work is fairly limited, but here they are used to great effect, and in the *Andantino*, the use of string glissandi (Britten's Midsummer Night's Dream perhaps?) darker woodwind unison, and brass and marimba colours, foreshadows an atmosphere redolent of his *Cornish Dances'* slow movement. Given the fact that the symphony was a response to the Notting Hill race riots of 1960, the seemingly good humoured nature of the fugal last movement takes on a decidedly sardonic tone, particularly with the clear proto-*Peterloo Overture* music toward the end of the work (itself a homage to another earlier civil disturbance).

The Fifth is probably my favourite symphony, possibly because I came to it very early and it was the first Arnold symphony score I ever owned. I think, simply, that there is very little wrong with it. It has all one would hope from this composer – melodies aplenty (kitschy or not), drive, ebullience and unease. That such a symphony should come out of such dark and personal events (the death of four friends and the end of his first marriage) astounds me. The harmonic writing is deftly judged, the scoring wonderfully evocative, and I sense the composer at the height of his powers, enjoying the demands of symphonic composition. I still listen to this work every so often, and am convinced by it every time.

For me, after the Fifth, the intensity starts to wane. In the Sixth, the first movement's RVW hues (viz. 4th and 6th Symphonies) and the tripartite second movement with initial *DSCH* motif (not to forget the central section's mock-pop approximation with ride cymbal, rim shot and tambourine) seem uneven. The third movement's overly repetitious form (a rondo?) with proto-trumpet concerto finale opening and cruel violin arpeggios (was he having fun at the fiddles' expense?) mean that this particular symphony doesn't quite make a cohesive whole for me.

The Seventh continues the three-movement formal structure, but its architecture suffers once more from an overuse of repeated ideas as in the Sixth. However, I sense a real development in harmonic intensity, and if anything, it is now closer to a Schnittke or Shostakovichian ethos than ever before. The large central movement is one of the most searching and ambiguous musical statements I think Arnold ever made, with a definite mood-change in colour and form. The cowbell punctuations before the climax is an emotionally riveting event followed by an equally memorable slinking away of the movement in bassoon and viola sul pont tones. It is one of my favourite Arnold symphonic movements. The final movement confirms my feeling that this is Arnold *through the looking glass*, no longer mock-heroic or cheeky, but now darkly troubled. One particular section highlights the interesting blend of harp and piccolo 'ancient air' over dissonant backgrounds, leading to a quasi Irish/ medieval 'ductia' occurring late in the movement. My only wish is that Arnold might have ended the symphony with the three cowbell hits and not the final repeating F octaves!

The Eighth Symphony, the only one to be commissioned and premiered by an American orchestra, is something of a return to the Arnold of old, and yet not without disjuncture. Echoes once more of *Peterloo* (with pipe and tabor references) and the Dance sets of the late 50s and 60s make an appearance, but with a much darker underpinning. I sense a feeling of "false bonhomous abandon" (as Dylan Thomas, another troubled artist once put it) beginning to infect Arnold's work. A sour note is never far away, and the atmosphere is saturated more with dread than delight. The central movement of the three has several sections that are minimally or unusually scored. These are distinct departures for Arnold I think; for example, the horn, tuba, timpani and harp quartet must be one of the strangest combinations in his output (the Grand Grand overture not withstanding!). The last movement starts perkily enough but then enters a barren landscape of monodies and duos that make the movement's closing presentation of the movement's main theme seem, alas, a little too glibly tacked on.

The Ninth Symphony, being the longest of all the symphonies, elicits, paradoxically, the fewest comments from me. Whilst there is the occasional glimmer or residue of Arnold's musical fingerprints, I have always felt that this work is not really a quintessence of thought, but a waning, an impoverishment of compositional assertion. The adjectives used by other commentators (bleak, sparse etc.) have never really convinced me, as the music just doesn't have the power of its symphonic predecessors. I've tried to get inside, but it is quite an impenetrable work. Although this is not Arnold's last work, even though he wished it to be, the sense that the composer is now running on empty – his mental state was precarious around this time – comes across strongly. Yet the humanity and fragility of the work also comes through with equal power. The *Four Irish Dances*, Op. 126 (1986, the same year as the symphony) suffers from the same malaise, yet two years later, the *Four Welsh Dances*, Op. 138 (1988) seems to have been written by a somewhat reinvigorated Arnold. Still, the real zest and spark has gone, replaced perhaps by something deeper and more despairing, if not ghostly or more tenuous.

If viewed as separate parts of a single musical thread, then the symphonies can be seen to chart the ebb and flow of a composer who knew how to write brilliantly and effectively for the medium, making many a grand statement along the way. Arnold was clearly a composer who relished full-bodied, broad, and emotionally-affecting music, and it is this that guarantees him the deep affection of generations of music lovers. The very best of Arnold – the dark, the grotesque, the *sankey*, the ludicrous, and the humorous, live in his 'autobiographical' symphonies. If they "speak in clichés" to quote the composer himself, then they are clichés that resonate emotionally with the listener. Such resonance is something any composer would give much to be able to achieve.

Nigel Hess

My great aunt, Dame Myra Hess, became internationally famous for organising the six-year series of lunchtime concerts at London's National Gallery during the Second World War – virtually the only classical music publicly available at that time for war-torn Londoners. She was not known as a champion of contemporary music, so it is a real surprise to see, tucked away amongst the programme listings for December 1944, the first performance of the 23-year-old Malcolm Arnold's Quintet for flute, violin, viola, horn and bassoon. I would love to have known what the Gallery audience made of it, accustomed as they were to their Beethoven and Mozart. It's a jolly piece, so one can only hope that spirits were suitably raised, even if the dissonances in the middle movement must have raised a few eyebrows.

Three weeks before the concert. Arnold had started his army training in Canterbury and was mortified when his request to attend the Quintet's première was refused. Not to be outwitted, his wife Sheila went down to Canterbury, threw some civilian clothes to Malcolm over a fence, and he made the concert (all composers need wives like Sheila). His CO was not best pleased.

As a fellow composer, I am fascinated by the very human stories which surround the creation of such extraordinary music. The writing of Arnold's symphonies is full of such insights. For example, it brings one up short to learn that much of the Seventh Symphony was written in William Walton's house on the Italian island of Ischia. Walton was nineteen years Arnold's senior, but their friendship had begun back in 1941 when Walton conducted the first performance of his Violin Concerto and Arnold was playing trumpet in the orchestra. Fast forward to 1973 and Arnold is sketching his symphony in a rented cottage only yards away from Walton and his wife Susana – surely one of the few cases in musical history where two near-contemporary composers are working together in such proximity. In typical Arnold fashion, the visit ended prematurely with Malcolm storming out after a titanic argument with his lifelong friend – and 'borrowing' the Waltons' car to leave the island on the next ferry. How tempting it would be to hear some of this in the angst of the symphony itself!

The tortuous history of the Ninth Symphony makes sobering reading for composing colleagues. It was meant to have its première in 1985, but due to Arnold's increasing ill-health it wasn't ready and funding was withdrawn. The symphony wasn't completed until late the following year, at which point both the BBC (who were to mount the first performance) and Arnold's own publisher baulked at the score which was so different from his previous symphonies. It was finally given its first performance in 1992, thanks to the championing of Sir Charles Groves. All this would be profoundly depressing for a composer in rude health, but given Arnold's fragile state during these years it must have been bewildering at best. To continue to create during such dark times was clearly Malcolm's lifeline, but the increasing incomprehension from trusted colleagues must have contributed to the downward spiral in which he found himself.

The Nine Symphonies remain extraordinary documents of a troubled life, telling us as much about Arnold the man as Arnold the composer. They represent an incredible journey.

Jon Lord

Gustav Mahler famously said that "The symphony must be like the world – it must embrace everything", and I feel strongly that he would not, and could not, have modified that view had he heard Sir Malcolm's Nine. In fact he would surely have endorsed them as exemplars of this belief. You can hear in these works a wonderful and absolutely personal freedom of expression plus an ingenuity and skill which go along beautifully with a sense of the sharing of emotions that is often quite overwhelming. Yes, they are often dark, but, alongside, they can also have a wonderful sense of humour, intrigue, passion and excitement. They are strongly argued, terse and virile, and then you get those tunes! When I heard my first Arnold symphony – the 6th – in 1969 (invaluably, this was under the baton of Malcolm himself and in rehearsal too, so I was able to 'see inside' this marvellous work) I was well and truly hooked, and over the years I have listened to them all many times, and continue to do so and to marvel at them. I am proud to say that I knew him a little and glad to say that I owe him a lot. British music owes him an enormous amount and he should be celebrated as one of the greats. When will we finally hear again one of these exceptional symphonies at The Proms?

David Matthews

Thoughts on the Second Symphony

Malcolm Arnold was a natural symphonist, and like Mahler and Shostakovich, he used the form to project the continuing drama of his own life. His First Symphony, with its violent shifts of mood, I find somewhat alarming, and Arnold never quite overcomes the inert desperation at the centre of the first movement. The Second Symphony, by contrast, is securely confident and altogether delightful. The clarinet theme with which it opens, in a serene E flat major, is instantly memorable and beautifully shaped (it is worth pointing out that none of the other British symphonists of his generation – Arnell, Fricker, Rawsthorne, Searle, etc. – could write memorable tunes like Arnold). Arnold repeats it twice, with increasing richness of texture; the theme is exactly the same each time, except that each repetition has a subtly different ending. In the development there are hints of Sibelius – whom Arnold acknowledged as the greatest single influence on his music – but they are subsumed within his, by now, completely personal style. The scherzo's hectic energy is never threatening, merely high-spirited. Similarly, the mood of tragedy in the slow movement – one of Arnold's finest achievements – is not allowed to get out of control, but remains dignified even at its darkest. A tolling bell introduces the central funeral procession, where Arnold comes close to Mahler but again remains indubitably himself. The finale is a striking example of the kind of uninhibited music in popular style at which Arnold excelled, even if, as Donald Mitchell pointed out, the continuation of the main tune is rather 'slovenly' – a consequence of Arnold's occasional inability, as music poured out of him, to be self-critical. It's a minor lapse: the music builds up to a triumphant E flat major ending which sounds absolutely genuine. How many composers in the 1950s could do that?

Arnold was 31 when he completed his Second Symphony, which consolidated his reputation as a major British composer. It is absurd that it isn't in the standard repertoire; it has all the necessary ingredients for popularity, and is superbly written. It's an instance of the particular difficulty this country has in giving due recognition to its composers.

John McCabe

Arnold Symphonies: A Do-It-Yourself Essay

When I was asked to contribute to the symposium on Malcolm Arnold's symphonies, I set about listening to them all, in chronological order, as the best way of sorting out my own feelings about them. Two (Nos 2 and 5) have been firm favourites for many years – there are others which I respect without having the same personal affection for them, and others by which I am only convinced in part. I found that during this process, some of my opinions changed a little but not radically – more pertinently, I found it impossible to define my own feelings about this body of works any more securely than before. I wrote most of a short essay about them before realising that I was getting more and more confused. So I decided to ask a series of questions, rather like an examination paper, which might help me resolve the problem. They haven't done so. However, in the hope that they cast some light on the symphonies by asking relevant questions, I decided my best way forward was simply to provide you, the reader, with them – there is no requirement to hand your papers in at the end of the test!

1. To what extent do extraneous circumstances affect a listener's assessment of a particular composer's music?

2. Is the 1st Symphony: (i) an apparently random, cheek-by-jowl assemblage of different, often seemingly unrelated elements, in a stream-of-consciousness technique, bearing no relation to conventional symphonic thought; (ii) an astonishing, almost stream-of-consciousness assemblage of fragments adding up to a major contribution to the development of symphonic form in a new direction; or (iii) an example of a composer finding his way experimentally into a genre to which he desperately wants to contribute?

3. In Robert Simpson's words, symphonies must "travel", they must be "dramatic as wholes...not dramatic in their internal processes." To what extent do Arnold's symphonies fulfil this requirement?

4. How successfully does Arnold integrate influences (e.g. Sibelius or Walton) into his own style? Sibelius is often quoted as one influence, but as Brahms said in a different context, "any fool can see that" – does it, for

example, vitiate the authority of, say, the 2nd Symphony to have passages of strongly Sibelian cast, or does Arnold's individuality remain in place?

5. Is the 9th Symphony a satisfactory conclusion to the cycle?

6. Do the Symphony for Strings (1946) and Symphony for Brass (1978) belong as an integral part of the series (making it eleven symphonies and not just nine numbered ones)?

7. Do the spare textures such as the bleak two-part counterpoint to be found in Nos 8 and 9 indicate a loss of creative energy or simply a paring-down to essentials?

8. What function do Arnold's characteristic ostinati (often just repetition of two notes, and often just a repetition of dominant-tonic) fulfil within his symphonic technique?

9. How, and how successfully, does Arnold use the vernacular within the context of a symphonic technique? (Examples would be the 'Caribbean' percussion in the 4th Symphony, the pop ballad given such massive importance at the climax of the 5th, or the influence of jazz on the first movement of the 6th.)

10. To what extent did Arnold's prolific output of film scores influence his symphonic music? Was it a positive or a negative influence (or, perhaps, neither)?

Please do not try to guess what my answers would be – well, you can of course have a go, but they are very inconsistent. Hence my initial problem! One thing remains constant, however, the fascination Arnold's music holds and its ability to lead to much discussion.

John McCabe – 14th April 2011

Matthew Taylor

Arnold the Symphonist

It is always difficult to assess the significance of a composer's work in the years immediately following his death. There tends to be a flurry of activity, sometimes including an intensive series of concerts, and then the long silence. With Malcolm Arnold the situation is different: his music was regularly performed during his lifetime and is still being programmed to a limited extent today. And even if some areas of the British Musical Establishment undervalued his genius there seems no danger that his work will disappear from the concert repertoire. The problem however is that his most representative works are either insufficiently known, undervalued or simply ignored by concert promoters.

The nine symphonies are undoubtedly amongst his most significant works, each of them, even the highly controversial No. 9, reveals the work of an exceptionally original symphonist, and one who can embrace powerful forces in a manner quite unlike any of his contemporaries. But whilst Arnold's language may appear outwardly quite traditional, and his forms fairly conventional, there is a very disturbing vein which runs through the cycle. The bleak Funeral March from No. 2, for instance, seems so bewildering in an otherwise predominantly sunny, genial symphony, yet it somehow works within the larger scope of the work. The destructive forces that literally threaten to break apart the expected jubilation at the end of No. 4 reveal all too vividly the conflicts of race riots at the Notting Hill Carnival in 1960. No wonder that most critics of the time simply 'didn't get it' – it was too provocative for them. But perhaps most original of all is the conclusion of No. 5, when the sumptuous slow movement tune returns in sweeping, big-hearted orchestration, only to freeze on a big minor-key chord so that everything heard in the symphony is suddenly revalued.

In Symphonies 6 to 8, Arnold seems to operate the system in reverse, so that the unsettling qualities are more often manifested by supposedly alien ideas introduced into the symphonic fabric – the snatch of nightclub melody which interrupts the gallows music in the central part of the 6th Symphony, or the little Irish tune which creeps bizarrely into the finale of the otherwise intensely black 7th Symphony, perhaps provoking the deliberately hollow triumph. But possibly the most brilliantly calculated of all is the innocent D major tune taken from a film score that saunters through the desolate landscape of the first movement of No. 8, seemingly unaffected or uncorrupted by the surrounding music.

In many ways the Ninth (1986), which many felt at the time was the most problematic of all, is unusual only through the almost total lack of disturbing elements which occurred in the earlier symphonies, for though textures are very spare indeed, the discourse is simple and the closing bars of the finale suggest a peace and sense of repose unique in the world of Arnold's symphonism. The prevailing criticisms of the work at the time focused upon its bare bones, the predominance of two-part writing, the big spans of inactivity. However, all these observations merely define the originality of the Ninth, whose directness of expression is so refreshing when the climate of so much contemporary music of the time swung in the other direction – dense, congested textures, scores of colour but little thematic substance – lots of notes doing little. And even if the Ninth does not reach the same level of mastery and intellectual strength as the Ninth of Arnold's exact contemporary, Robert Simpson, also completed in 1986, it still stands as one of the most important 20th century symphonies.

I can think of few things in post-war British music more necessary and more exciting than a complete cycle of the Arnold symphonies, and I congratulate all who are involved in this magnificent project.

John Woolrich

What we want from composers above all is honesty. We don't want them to censor their imaginations, particularly on the grounds of good taste. Malcolm Arnold strikes me as being an entirely honest composer. Without knowing the man, you could reconstruct the personality from his music.

When Arnold does something – whether it's tender or blustering, lushly melodious or dryly motivic, dark or light, Mahlerian or music hall – he takes it to extremes. It's big-boned music, clear and direct, and open-hearted. There's little attempt to soften the edges: the juxtapositions between different worlds can be raw and unpredictable. It's flawed music no doubt, but so much the better for that – real art grows in the cracks and dark spaces.